The Forgotten Heavens

THE forgotten HEAVENS

Six Essays on Cosmology

edited by **DOUGLAS WILSON**

TERRY MORIN | EVAN WILSON | GREG DICKISON

CHRISTOPHER SCHLECT | WESLEY CALLIHAN

canonpress
Moscow, Idaho

Published by Canon Press
P.O. Box 8729, Moscow, ID 83843
800.488.2034 | www.canonpress.com

The Forgotten Heavens: Six Essays on Cosmology
Copyright © 1989, 2010 by Canon Press.

All Scripture quotations are taken from the Authorized Version unless otherwise noted.

Cover illustration: Detail of *The Fall of the Rebel Angels*, Frans Floris, oil on canvas, 1554.
Cover and interior design by Laura Storm.
Printed in the United States of America.

Library of Congress Cataloging-in-Publication Data

The forgotten heavens : six essays on cosmology / Douglas Wilson, editor ; [contributions by] Terry Morin [... et al.].
    p. cm.
 ISBN-13: 978-1-59128-071-2 (pbk.)
 ISBN-10: 1-59128-071-0 (pbk.)
 1. Biblical cosmology. 2. Angels. 3. Demonology. I. Wilson, Douglas, 1953- II. Morin, Terry. III. Title.
 BS651.F68 2010
 235'.4--dc22

                                        2010001014

10 11 12 13 14 15 16 17   9 8 7 6 5 4 3 2

To our wives & children

CONTENTS

PREFACE

It is regrettable that evangelical Christians are not always to be trusted when it comes to handling the Scriptures. Those who should be the staunchest defenders of the Word of God against all comers are sometimes not. And why is this?

On some issues, the theological liberal is better able to state what the teaching of the Bible is. This is because he is able to say that, for example, the apostle Paul thought this way, and wasn't it quaint? The evangelical, on the other hand, is required to *believe* whatever Paul taught in the Scriptures; the conservative is stuck with the results of his exegesis. Therefore, if Paul taught anything that is extremely out of step with modern prejudices, that aspect of his teaching must be ignored, or at least reinterpreted.

For example: Evangelicals do believe in the spiritual realm, but they have divorced that realm from the world we actually live in. Angels, or spirits, are in another dimension somewhere. But the Bible teaches that "He makes his angels winds, his servants flames of fire" (Heb. 1:7; Ps. 104:4).

But aren't winds just the motion of molecules in the air? This answer of the scientists is of course true, but it is not *exhaustive*. We have to be careful to avoid the fallacy of reductionism; what Donald Mackay calls "nothing buttery." The materialist can point out that a human being is made up of the following chemicals, and then list them all. Within this list, he does not find the constituent parts of a soul, or a spirit. Do they therefore not exist? The Christian answers clearly—the soul cannot be analyzed in that way. Hamlet is "nothing but" paper and ink, and yet we rightly feel that such an account of it leaves out the most important part.

But why do we defend God's creation from the materialist at only the point of man's dignity? He says that we are "nothing but" certain chemicals, and we beg to differ. He then says that the winds are "nothing but" atoms in motion, and we, for some strange reason, agree. He says that stars are "nothing but" flaming balls of gas, and we agree with this as well.

Now the Bible does not teach that all winds are necessarily angels. We are not required to believe that there is no such thing as an inanimate object. But the Bible does teach that there is intelligence behind many things that the modern materialist dismisses as "processes," "forces," or just plain "matter."

Man is not rattling around inside a big empty universe. The Creator of all is not an impersonal force, and the creation reflects that. The biblical view of the cosmos is not the one of modernity—infinite depths of lifeless space punctuated by dead rock, or chaotic fire. On the contrary, the universe is filled with intelligence and life.

The New Bible Dictionary confirms this observation:

> [T]he implied angelology of C. S. Lewis's novels (*Out of the Silent Planet*, etc.) would probably have commended itself with some force to the biblical writers. The Bible certainly suggests that angels of different ranks have charge of individuals and of nations; no doubt in the light of modern cosmology this concept, if retained, at all (as biblically it must be), ought properly to be extended, as the dual sense of the phrase "Host of Heaven" suggests, to the oversight of the elements of the physical universe—planets, stars, and nebulae.[1]

In fact, the only difference between what we are doing here in this symposium, and what C. S. Lewis did—apart from his

1. J. D. Douglas, ed., *The New Bible Dictionary* (Grand Rapids: Eerdmans, 1962), 543.

talent—is found in the fact that he had the good sense to put his convictions on such subjects into his fiction.

Some of the examples of evangelical revisionism would be tragic if they were not so funny. In the book of Job, God is describing some of the great creatures He has made. About the Behemoth, He says this:

> Look at the behemoth, which I made along with you and which feeds on grass like an ox. What strength he has in his loins, what power in the muscles of his belly! His tail sways like a cedar. (Job 40:15–17a)

The NIV provides us with an informative footnote which explains that this may possibly be the hippopotamus or elephant—with a tail like a cedar. Apparently the scholars who worked on the NIV were too busy with their studies as children, and never made it to the zoo, or the circus.

Examples could be multiplied, but that is the job undertaken in the following essays. The reader is encouraged to approach the biblical arguments presented here with an open mind, and with an open commitment to the inerrant Word of God.

The first essay is mine, and it addresses the broad subject of the heavens and the underworld. Terry Morin is the author of the second essay, in which he discusses the various manifestations of God's throne in the Bible, along with certain attendants to that throne.

Evan Wilson addresses the government of princes, and shows how the nations of the Old Testament era were governed by spiritual princes. The next essay is on divination and witchcraft, and was written by Greg Dickison. This is followed by Chris Schlect's contribution, which is on the ever-popular subject of angels. Finally, Wes Callihan shows how materialistic assumptions can affect translation, and not just interpretation. His essay is on the Bible's references to satyrs.

All of the essays except the last one were presented at the Community Evangelical Fellowship (CEF) Symposium on Cosmology in the spring of 1989, in Moscow, Idaho. As you read this book, we hope our desire to be biblical is clear to you throughout; where it has not been obvious, we beg your pardon in advance. At the same time, we hope you enjoy learning some things you never learned in Sunday School.

DOUGLAS WILSON

1

THE HEAVENS, HADES,
& MAN BETWEEN

Douglas Wilson

The task we have set for ourselves in this essay is to take a tour of the biblical cosmos—a sort of biblical cosmography, if you like. As we begin, we need to recognize that we will have to cover a great deal of territory, and that we must lighten our loads considerably. Perhaps the best things to leave behind, at least for the time being, are our prejudices. For, as C. S. Lewis pointed out in *The Allegory of Love*, the present must also be recognized as a "period." When we consider that future scholars will one day be studying our quaint notions, it will perhaps supply us with necessary humility as we study the past. The need for such humility is even greater when we consider that, as Christians, we possess a divinely inspired book which contains in it many assumptions which are not shared by the natives of modernity.

As we proceed, it will become clear that we must rethink our assumptions about the universe around us.

But if we submit to the biblical cosmology, it will not be found necessary to submit to a caricature of it—we are not living in a universe built like a three-decker London bus, riding on the back of a turtle. Nothing said here conflicts with what modem scientists know scientifically to be true. It does conflict, however, with a good deal of modern pseudo-scientific speculation.

It is necessary to make this point because it is easy for modern men to dismiss the ancients as primitives and to reject as nonsense the idea of the heavens above, and Hades below. To that idea we now turn.

The Supremacy of Christ

> Therefore God exalted him to the highest place and gave him the name that is above every name, that at the name of Jesus every knee should bow, in heaven and on earth and under the earth, and every tongue confess that Jesus Christ is Lord, to the glory of God the Father. (Phil. 2:9–11, cf. Rev. 5:3)

Paul is telling us here that the supremacy of Jesus Christ will one day be acknowledged by all, everywhere. His authority extends to every nook and cranny of the universe; to the heavens above, to the earth we live on, and to the Underworld, or Hades. In the Greek, he is not referring to these three places, but, rather to the creatures inhabiting them, i.e., heavenly creatures, earthly creatures, and subterranean creatures.

As Jesus tells His disciples in the Great Commission, all authority is His, whether it is in heaven or on earth. The authority of Christ is completely universal, and includes all the forces of wickedness. The One who saw Satan fall like lightning from heaven has triumphed over all power and authority through His cross and resurrection (Lk. 10:17–20).

> For in Christ all the fullness of the Deity lives in bodily form, and you have been given fullness in Christ, who is the head over every power and authority ... And having disarmed the powers and authorities, he made a public spectacle of them, triumphing over them by the cross. (Col. 2:9–10, 15)

The significance of this triumph was not lost on the early Christians. They knew that they were partakers of that triumph, and that Satan would soon be crushed under their feet (Rom. 16:20).

So Jesus did not die in order to set an ethical dualism in stone, with God and Satan forever opposed. He spoke of the condemnation of the prince of this world (Jn. 16:7–11); He appeared in order to destroy the devil's work (1 Jn. 3:8); He died to destroy the devil himself (Heb. 2:14); and He stated that in His death the prince of the world would be driven out (Jn. 12:29–32).

As we examine the biblical cosmology, we should keep in mind that we are studying, because of the resurrection, the domain of Christ. Nothing is outside that domain. Let us begin with Heaven, or as the biblical writers frequently would have it, the heavens.[1]

The Glory of God

> Is not God in the heights of heaven? And see how lofty are the highest stars! (Job 22:12)

> God, the blessed and only Ruler, the King of kings and Lord of lords, who alone is immortal and who lives in unapproachable light, whom no one has seen or can see. To him be honor and might forever. Amen. (1 Tim. 6:15–16)

The Bible teaches that God's glorious presence is manifested beyond the highest stars, and that He dwells in light that cannot be approached. This is not a limitation of God's glory or presence, for He is omnipresent, i.e., everywhere. As the Scriptures so clearly declare, not even the heavens contain Him. "But will God really

---

1. The heavens. In Matthew, 76% of the references to heaven are plural in the original; in Mark only 29% are plural; in Luke, 12% are plural; in John, 100% are singular; in Acts, 9% are plural; in the epistles it is 50/50; and in Revelation, all the references are singular.

dwell on earth? The heavens, even the highest heaven, cannot contain you. How much less this temple I have built!" (1 Kgs. 8:27).

Nevertheless, God's glory is manifested beyond the stars, and it is a place where creatures are undone. He has set His glory above the heavens (Ps. 8:1; 113:4–6). He must stoop down to look at the heavens.

The Bible does not identify beyond question where this is. What direction is it? Surely it is not sufficient to simply point "up." With the information we have, we can only offer a suggestion, but it is worth considering as a possibility.

> Out of the north he comes in golden splendor; God comes in awesome majesty. (Job 37:22; cf. Job 26:7)

> Great is the Lord, and most worthy of praise, in the city of our God, his holy mountain. It is beautiful in its loftiness, the joy of the whole earth. Like the utmost heights of Zaphon is Mount Zion, the city of the Great King. (Ps. 48:1–2)

In this second quotation, Mount Zion is compared favorably to Zaphon, the "Olympus" of Baal. Zaphon's connection with the north can be clearly seen when you consider the KJV translation of this—is Mt. Zion on the sides of the north." Zaphon *means* north.

This term "Zaphon" shows up again in Isaiah 14, in the boast of the king of Babylon: "I will raise my throne above the stars of God; I will sit enthroned on the mount of assembly, on the utmost heights of the north" (v. 13b).

Another passage, this one in the Psalms, shows the connection between God and the north. "No one from the east or the west or from the desert [south] can exalt a man. But it is God who judges: He brings one down, He exalts another" (Ps. 75:6–7).

The implication here is clear. No one from east, west or south can determine who is exalted and who not. That can only be done by the one from the north.

In Ezekiel 1:4, the vision of God that comes to Ezekiel, comes to him out of the north.

As we consider these passages, we can see that if any direction is associated in Scripture with the majesty of God, it is the north.

The Heavens

God is the Creator of all things and this includes the stars—the starry host were made by the breath of His mouth (Ps. 33:6). As Creator, God's knowledge of the stars is detailed—for example, He calls them each by name (Is. 40:26; Ps. 147:4). Among the greatest of creatures, the multitudes of heaven worship God as their Creator (Neh. 9:6; Ps. 148:3).

To say that stars worship God is not just a figure of speech—the stones crying out and so forth. We can see clearly that the heavenly host, what we call stars, are personal. They have intelligence. For example, when Micaiah sees his vision of the throne of God, the host of heaven are the heavenly courtiers.

> Micaiah continued, "Therefore hear the word of the Lord: I saw the Lord sitting on his throne with all the host of heaven standing around him on his right and on his left." (1 Kgs. 22:19; cf. 2 Chr. 18:18)

We may also see the intelligence of the heavenly host in a very familiar story—perhaps too familiar. The night Jesus was born, the shepherds who came to see Jesus were guarding their flocks by night. They were informed of the Messiah's birth by a choir of stars, which are also identified as angels (v. 15).

> Suddenly a great company of the heavenly host appeared with the angel, praising God and saying, "Glory to God in the highest, and on earth peace to men on whom his favor rests." (Lk. 2:13–14)

Done with their song, the stars receded back into their usual station in the heavens.

When the eastern wise men came to find Jesus, they were guided to a particular house by a star (Mt. 2:9). Either the star came down into our atmosphere the same way the choir of stars had, or the Magi were profound astrologers indeed. I prefer the former explanation, but in either case it is clear that stars are not just flaming balls of gas. It is also clear that the intelligence associated with a star can transform its body, or separate from it, in order to do things like this. A star which came down without such a separation would fry our planet to a cinder.

At the same time, we need to remember that this truth about the stars cannot be used as a justification for pagan or superstitious astrology. The Bible is clear, and severe, in its condemnation of such astrological practices. We may also exclude as unbiblical the tomfoolery printed in modern newspaper horoscopes.

Still, the Magi were probably astrologers, and Daniel was the chief of all the astrologers in Babylon (Dan. 5:11).

The heavenly host are described as being servants of God, who do His will (Ps. 103:21). They are capable of praising God, just like the angels (Ps. 148:2). But even with all their greatness, they do not compare with the Lord (Ps. 89:6). God is described as their Father (Jas. 1:17). They can be compared with man, and for the time being anyway, they are a little greater (Ps. 8:5).

The apostle Paul clearly refers to the stars as beings. He says: "There are also heavenly bodies and there are earthly bodies; but the splendor of the heavenly bodies is one kind, and the splendor of the earthly bodies is another" (1 Cor. 15:40).

In defining the word Paul uses here, Thayer says that it refers to "the bodies of the stars (which the apostle, according to the universal ancient conception, seems to have regarded as animate."[2]

2. Thayer, *Thayer's Greek-English Lexicon of the New Testament* (New York: American Book Company, 1886), 247.

The New Jerusalem

The New Jerusalem is not the same thing as heaven, but it necessary to say a few things about it here.

This is because much of the imagery we have of heaven comes, not from the biblical descriptions of heaven, but from the descriptions of the New Jerusalem—pearly gates, streets of gold, and so forth. This confusion is perpetuated principally through hymns and cartoons.

The New Jerusalem is a biblical metaphor for the Christian church—both on earth and in heaven. This identification is not speculation—it is explicitly made in Scripture.

For example, John is told by one of the seven angels that he will be shown "the bride, the wife of the Lamb" (Rev. 21:9), which is of course the Christian church (Eph. 5:25–27). And what is John shown? "The Holy City, Jerusalem, coming down out of heaven from God" (Rev. 21:10).

In the Book of Hebrews, the saints are told that they have not come to a physical city—to one that can be touched.

> You have not come to a mountain that can be touched and that is burning with fire; to darkness, gloom and storm; to a trumpet blast or to such a voice speaking words that those who heard it begged that no further word be spoken to them, because they could not bear what was commanded: "If even an animal touches the mountain, it must be stoned." The sight was so terrifying that Moses said, "I am trembling with fear."
>
> But you have come to Mount Zion, to the heavenly Jerusalem, the city of the living God. You have come to thousands upon thousands of angels in joyful assembly, to the church of the firstborn, whose names are written in heaven. You have come to God, the judge of all men, to the spirits of righteous men made perfect, to Jesus the mediator of a new covenant, and to the sprinkled blood that speaks a better word than the blood of Abel. (Heb. 12:18–24)

They had been converted; they were saints of God; they had already come, by faith, to the new Jerusalem.

This understanding is confirmed when Paul talks about the New Jerusalem in Galatians (Gal. 4:24–31). Consequently, for the sake of accuracy we must be careful not to apply the details of a symbolic image of the church to our final glorious state after the resurrection. They are two different things.

The Stars and Men

The stars are not removed from the affairs of men, particularly men who govern nations. When the king of Babylon was swollen in his arrogance, he thought: "I will ascend to heaven; I will raise my throne above the stars of God; I will sit enthroned on the mount of assembly, on the utmost heights of the sacred mountain" (Is. 14:13).

This is not mere arrogance. The possibility of a human ruler being able to do this should not be excluded. In Daniel 8, Daniel describes the growth of the power of Antiochus Epiphanes in this way:

> It grew until it reached the host of the heavens, and it threw some of the starry host down to the earth and trampled on them. It set itself up to be as great as the Prince of the host; it took away the daily sacrifice from him, and the place of his sanctuary was brought low. (Dan. 8:10–11)

Notice that when his power grew, he trampled on some of the starry host, and thought himself to be as great as an unnamed Prince of the host of heaven. In addition, when Sisera was destroyed in the Book of Judges, the stars were said to have had a role in it. "From the heavens the stars fought, from their courses they fought against Sisera" (Judg. 5:20).

It is worth noting here the martial connotations of the word "host" in the phrase "host of heaven." We are talking about the armies of heaven. Remember how Satan fell from heaven; he was thrown down as a result of a lost battle with Michael (Rev. 12:7). There was war in heaven. We can also see this martial aspect in Christ's reference to "legions" of angels.

In the Book of Isaiah, the prophet clearly links the powers above, and the kings beneath. He says:

> In that day the Lord will punish the powers in the heavens above and the kings on the earth below. They will be herded together like prisoners bound in a dungeon; they will be shut up in prison and be punished after many days." (Is. 24:21–22)

It is also true that the destruction of various nations is set out in different prophecies in terms of a collapsing universe and solar system. These prophecies do deal with mundane political realities, but they are not just another way of telling some king that "his lights are going to go out." His destruction is accompanied by a destruction in the heavens—the fall from power of certain celestials.

Isaiah prophesies against Babylon and Edom in this way (Is. 13:1, 10; 34:4–5), and Jesus picks up his language to prophesy the destruction of Jerusalem in A.D. 70 (Mt. 24:29, see also Lk. 21:25–26; Mk. 13:25) Ezekiel prophecies with this, type of terminology against Pharaoh, King of Egypt (Ezek. 32:2, 7). The prophet Amos declares judgment against the northern kingdom of Israel in a very similar way (Amos 8:2, 9). And of course, the quotation by Peter at Pentecost of Joel's prophecy against Israel fits into this pattern (Joel 2:30–31; Acts 2:17–21). This is also a probable interpretation of the prophecies in Revelation 6:13 and 8:12.

This type of language is also used in Scripture to show the changes brought about by the kingdom of God.

> At that time his voice shook the earth, but now he has promised, "Once more I will shake not only the earth but also the heavens." The words "once more" indicate the removing of what

can be shaken—that is, created things—so that what cannot be shaken may remain. (Heb. 12:26–27)

An understanding of all this is important to a right understanding of spiritual warfare. In Ephesians 1:20, we learn that Christ has been seated at the right hand of the Father in the heavenly realms. We, as Christians, are seated there in Christ (Eph. 1:3; 2:6). God has manifested His wisdom through the gospel, and that manifested wisdom is for the benefit of rulers and authorities in the heavenly realms. After teaching us this, Paul goes on to tell us that we are involved in a spiritual war against spiritual entities, both here and in the heavens.

> For our struggle is not against flesh and blood, but against the rulers, against the authorities, against the powers of this dark world and against the spiritual forces of evil in the heavenly realms. (Eph. 6:12)

All too often, Christians reduce spiritual warfare to techniques of prayer, or methodologies of witnessing. But it clearly involves more—devils below, and celestials above. Our prayers, and our preaching, have an effect that transcends our earthly limitations. This great authority is exercised only in Christ.

The Great Temptation

The glory of the heavenly host is such that there has been, down through history, a real temptation for sinful men to worship them. All such worship is forbidden by God.

> And when you look up to the sky and see the sun, the moon and the stars—all the heavenly array—do not be enticed into bowing down to them and worshiping things the Lord your God has apportioned to all the nations under heaven. (Deut. 4:19; cf. Deut. 17:3)

But of course, given the nature of man, this command was not obeyed, and we have good reason to think that some of the stars participated in the disobedience, and received the idolatrous worship.

> If even the moon is not bright and the stars are not pure in his eyes, how much less man, who is but a maggot—a son of man, who is only a worm! (Job 25:5–6)

One example of this is the worship of Molech, and the associated worship of Rephan. Stephen mentions this in Acts 7:43, when he quotes Amos 5:26. He says:

> But God turned away and gave them over to the worship of the heavenly bodies [the host of heaven]. This agrees with what is written in the book of the prophets:
> "Did you bring me sacrifices and offerings forty years in the desert, O house of Israel? You have lifted up the shrine of Moloch and the star of your god Rephan, the idols you made to worship. Therefore I will send you into exile beyond Babylon." (Acts 7:42–43)

Rephan is a god associated with the planet Saturn.[3] Molech, the god of the Ammonites (1 Kgs. 11:5), is clearly identified with worship of the starry host.

> [T]hose who bow down on the roofs to worship the starry host, those who bow down and swear by the Lord and who also swear by Molech. (Zeph. 1:5)

In addition, Isaiah links Molech to Sheol, the place of the departed dead (Is. 57:9). That the worship of this god was vile can be seen in Jeremiah's condemnation.

---

3. J. D. Douglas, ed., *The New Bible Dictionary* (Grand Rapids: Eerdmans, 1962), 1083.

They built high places for Baal in the Valley of Ben Hinnom to sacrifice their sons and daughters to Molech, though I never commanded, nor did it enter my mind, that they should do such a detestable thing and so make Judah sin (Jer. 32:35; see also 2 Kgs. 23:10; the worship of the starry host was also associated with Baal; see 2 Kgs. 17:16–17).

Another example was the worship of Ishtar, identified by Jeremiah as the Queen of Heaven (Jer. 44:17–18).

The Sons of God

The question of evil in the heavenly places is not a question of mere academic interest to men. The greatest cataclysm that has ever befallen our race was the result of celestial beings not keeping to their appointed habitation.

In Genesis 6, we find an account given of the Deluge, and of the reasons for it. It was because the "sons of God," or *bene elohim*, saw that human women were fair, married them, and had children by them.

Everywhere else this phrase appears in the Bible, it refers to celestial beings (Job 1:6; 2:1; 38:7, and in the singular, Dan. 3:25). From the references in the first part of Job, we find that Satan is one of their number, or at least accompanies them. In Job 38, these sons of Elohim are distinguished from the morning stars.

It appears that these sons of Elohim are also referred to as the Nephalim (or "fallen ones"), and their offspring are called the same after them. In Numbers 13:33, the unbelieving spies reported that there were Nephalim in the land (this, unlike Genesis 6, was after the Flood). There is an editorial comment which states that the descendents of Anak came from the Nephalim. From this we see that the half-breed descendants took their name from their celestial ancestors, and that this particular sin was not limited to the antediluvian era (which provides us with a possible explanation of the warning in 1 Corinthians 11:10).

Jude verifies that these beings did not keep their proper station, and that the nature of their sin was sexual. He states clearly that the inhabitants of Sodom and Gomorrah sinned in the same way as these beings, by going after strange flesh (v. 6–7).

That some bodily metamorphoses was involved can be seen in Jude's use of the word *oiketerion*. The only other place it is used in the New Testament is in 2 Corinthians 5:2, where Paul is talking about the believer's desire to be clothed with a heavenly dwelling, or resurrection body.

This also provides us with a good explanation for the many pagan mythological stories which deal with human women having intercourse with various gods.

Greek mythology also testifies to the results of such an unnatural union. In Genesis, the result was the "mighty men of old." In Greek mythology, the children of gods and human women were called the Titans. They rebelled against the gods, lost the battle, and were locked up in Tartarus. The same thing probably happened to the Nephalim, as we shall see later.

In the New Testament, another name for these "sons of Elohim" is *doxas*, or literally, "glories." It is translated as "celestial beings" in Jude, as well as 2 Peter. We may make the identification on this basis: Satan is numbered among the "sons of Elohim" in the Old Testament, and he is reckoned as a "glory" in the New. Jude condemns those who, without any sense, revile these celestials (Jude 8–10; 2 Pet. 2:10). He then points out that not even Michael the archangel would do such a thing in his conflict with the devil, although, as Peter tells us, angels are stronger and more powerful. Hence, the devil is one of the celestials whom we ought not to revile.

It is important to remember this prohibition of reviling. Some Christians, in the heat of ignorant zeal, have thought that the fact of spiritual warfare allows us to mock and taunt. It does not.

Sheol

Sheol is the Hebrew term for the place of the departed dead. It called by a number of names; Sheol, the pit, and the Abyss in the Old Testament, and Hades in the Greek New Testament. One of the evil beings associated with this place was Abaddon (place of destruction), or in the Greek, Apollyon, meaning destroyer (Rev. 9:11).

This place of the dead does not exist on some other spiritual plane; it is below our feet—subterranean. Or, to put it another way, it is down (Prov. 15:24; Num. 16:30). It is also frequently associated with the ocean, or the deep. For example, in Job 26:5–6 we find: "The dead are in deep anguish, those beneath the waters and all that live in them. Sheol is naked before God; Abaddon lies uncovered."

Moffat's translation of this is really interesting. The word rendered as "dead" in the NIV is Rephaim.[4] "Before Him the primeval giants writhe, under the ocean in their prison; the underworld lies open to His eyes."

Some other passages that link Sheol with the ocean are Ezekiel 28:8, Psalm 69:14–15, and Jonah 2:1–6.

In checking some of these references, please be aware that the NIV has rendered Sheol as "the grave" in quite a few places. This is one of many examples of modern evangelicals attempting to make the biblical cosmology palatable to the modern materialist. Like all forms of spiritual compromise, it doesn't work. The materialists remain unimpressed, and we have abandoned what the Bible plainly teaches. There were perfectly good words for "grave" which could have been used had that been the intention of the biblical writers. Ezekiel graphically makes the point that the pit is located

---

4. In Deuteronomy 2:21, the Rephaim are compared in stature to these Anakim, suggesting perhaps a relation. The fact that the Valley of Rephaim is near the Valley of Ben Hinnom is also suggestive. The word is also used in a number of Old Testament passages to refer to "ghosts of the dead." But which dead?

in the earth below. It is not in another dimension somewhere; it is underneath our feet.

> Then I will bring you down with those who go down to the pit, to the people of long ago. I will make you dwell in the earth below, as in ancient ruins, with those who go down to the pit, and you will not return or take your place in the land of the living. I will bring you to a horrible end and you will be no more. You will be sought, but you will never again be found, declares the Sovereign Lord. (Ezek. 26:20–21)

The Bible also teaches that Sheol is a region of darkness. It is not a place where the sun rises. Job anticipates going to this land of the dead.

> Are not my few days almost over? Turn away from me so I can have a moment's joy before I go to the place of no return, to the land of gloom and deep shadow, to the land of deepest night, of deep shadow and disorder, where even the light is like darkness. (Job 10:20–22)

In the Old Testament, even God's people expected to go to Sheol when they died. For example, Samuel came up out of the ground when Saul went to the witch at Endor (1 Sam. 28:13–15), and Jacob expected to descend to Sheol (Gen. 37: 35). But even though Job, godly man, spoke this way about Sheol, he also had a hope that looked beyond the land of shadows. He said: "I know that my Redeemer lives, and that in the end he will stand upon the earth, and after my skin has been destroyed, yet in my flesh I will see God" (Job 19:25–26).

Although it is a region of death, national and tribal identities are retained. Ezekiel gives us a long macabre description of departed kings receiving a newcomer (Ezek. 32:17–32). Isaiah does something very similar. He describes how the king of Babylon will be received into Sheol—with a sort of majestic, gruesome pomp.

All your pomp has been brought down to Sheol, along with the noise of your harps; maggots are spread out beneath you and worms cover you. How you have fallen from heaven, O morning star, son of the dawn! You have been cast down to the earth, you who once laid low the nations! You said in your heart, "I will ascend to heaven; I will raise my throne above the stars of God; I will sit enthroned on the mount of assembly, on the utmost heights of the sacred mountain. I will ascend above the tops of the clouds; I will make myself like the Most High." But you are brought down to Sheol, to the depths of the pit. (Is. 14:11–15)

This prophecy, incidentally, has nothing to do with Satan, although for some mysterious reason it is frequently applied to him. Notice also that the prophecy is directed at an earthly king, who is represented as falling from heaven, and is described as the morning star. Jesus uses a similar kind of language in His prophecy, although He uses the Greek term—Hades.

And you, Capernaum, will you be lifted up to the skies? No, you will go down to Hades. If the miracles that were performed in you had been performed in Sodom, it would have remained to this day. (Mt. 11:23; cf. Lk. 10:15–16)

Incidentally, it is possible that Hades is the name, not only of this place, but also the name of its ruler (Rev. 6:8). In addition, the Abyss was a place that demons obviously considered undesirable (Lk. 8:31). In the Book of Revelation, Hades is frequently referred to as the Abyss (Rev. 9:1–2; 11:7; 17:8; 20:1, 3).

Jesus in Hades

Where did Jesus go when He died? The Apostles' Creed says that He "descended into hell." Is this accurate?

We have a number of clues in different parts of the Scripture. During the three days His body was in the tomb, we know that He was in Paradise with the repentant thief who asked to be remembered (Lk. 23:43), He was in the heart of the earth (Mt. 12:40), and that He preached to the spirits who had been rebellious at the time of Noah (1 Pet. 3:18–20). Putting these all together may not be as difficult as it initially appears.

One of the biblical passages the New Testament Christians cited in support of the resurrection of Christ was Psalm 16:8–11. It is quoted by Peter in Acts 2:25–28, and by Paul in Acts 13:35. The point they made with the quotation was not that the Christ would not go to Hades, but that He would not be abandoned there.

This is also a place where we can establish the biblical connection between Sheol and Hades. In the Hebrew in Psalm 16, the word is Sheol. In the Greek quotations in Acts, it is rendered as Hades.

> Therefore my heart is glad and my tongue rejoices; my body also will rest secure, because you will not abandon me to Sheol, nor will you let your Holy One see decay. You have made known to me the path of life; you will fill me with joy in your presence, with eternal pleasures at your right hand. (Ps. 16:9–11)

We can see here that the Messiah would spend some time in Sheol, the place of the dead, but that He would not be there long enough for His body to decay. By virtue of His resurrection, Jesus conquered death and Hades. He conquered it because He went there, and came back, never to die again. "I am the Living One; I was dead, and behold I am alive for ever and ever! And I hold the keys of death and Hades" (Rev. 1:18).

We know therefore that Jesus went to Hades, which is in the heart of the earth. This accounts for His statement in Matthew 12 (as well as teaching us where the Lord thought Hades to be), but what about the reference to Paradise? And when did He preach to the spirits in prison?

Before answering the question, it is necessary to understand something about the structure of Hades. According to Greek mythology, Hades had two compartments. The dead who had lived a good life went to that part of Hades called Elysium. It was still a land of shadows, but it was not a place of torment.

In Luke 16, Jesus told a story which shows that there was no great difference between the Jewish idea and this Greek conception of Hades.

> There was a rich man who was dressed in purple and fine linen and lived in luxury every day. At his gate was laid a beggar named Lazarus, covered with sores and longing to eat what fell from the rich man's table. Even the dogs came and licked his sores.
>
> The time came when the beggar died and the angels carried him to Abraham's side. The rich man also died and was buried. In Hades, where he was in torment, he looked up and saw Abraham far away, with Lazarus by his side. So he called to him, "Father Abraham, have pity on me and send Lazarus to dip the tip of his finger in water and cool my tongue, because I am in agony in this fire."
>
> But Abraham replied, "Son, remember that in your lifetime you received your good things, while Lazarus received bad things, but now he is comforted here and you are in agony. And besides all this, between us and you a great chasm has been fixed, so that those who want to go from here to you cannot, nor can anyone cross over from there to us.'
>
> He answered, "Then I beg you, father, send Lazarus to my father's house, for I have five brothers. Let him warn them, so that they will not also come to this place of torment."
>
> Abraham replied, "They have Moses and the Prophets; let them listen to them."
>
> "No, father Abraham," he said, "but if someone from the dead goes to them, they will repent.
>
> He said to him, "If they do not listen to Moses and the Prophets, they will not be convinced even if someone rises from the dead." (Lk. 16:19–31)

Some have thought to escape the force of Jesus' teaching here by pointing out that Jesus was teaching through a parable. His point was obviously that a resurrection from the dead (and He had His own in view) would not convince someone who disregarded Moses and the prophets. This is quite true, but there are two other points to consider.

The first is relatively minor and concerns Christ's use of proper names, which He does not do in His other parables. In them, it is "a certain man . . ."

Secondly, given that it was a parable, how does it follow that a reference to Hades in a parable means nothing? Shall we argue that because Jesus was using a parable when He said, "A man was going down from Jerusalem to Jericho . . ." that we are not required to believe that Jerusalem and Jericho existed?

We may derive from Jesus' teaching, therefore, three basic points about Hades.

1. Part of it was a place of torment, and that it is the part reserved for the wicked.
2. Part of it was a place of comfort, and that Lazarus was there, along with Abraham, an Old Testament saint.
3. The two compartments were separated by an chasm which could not be crossed.

So when Jesus told the thief on the cross that they would be together in Paradise, He was referring to that place of comfort, in Hades, where Abraham was. From that place, He preached to the spirits who had been disobedient at the time of Noah. The word used for "preach" in Peter is not the word that refers to the preaching of the gospel. Rather, Jesus is simply announcing something, which I believe to be a pronouncement of their final defeat.

Who were these spirits? I believe they were the Nephalim who intermarried with human women, and possibly the Nephalim, their offspring. In Greek mythology, as was mentioned earlier, they were known as the Titans.

Where were they? They were in Tartarus, which was the lowest pit of Hades. It is at least possible that this is the chasm that separated Paradise from the place of torment. In Greek mythology, the Titans were in Tartarus because of their rebellion against the gods. In the biblical picture, they are there because of their rebellion against God.

In the ancient Greek cosmology, Tartarus was the pit of Hades. In the *Iliad*, Jove threatens the other gods, lest they help the Trojans. "I will hurl him down into dark Tartarus far into the deepest pit under the earth, where the gates are iron and the floor bronze, as far beneath Hades as heaven is high above the earth" (*Iliad*, Book 8).

Peter refers to this place by name, and does not feel that it is necessary to redefine it in anyway. "For if God did not spare angels when they sinned, but sent them to Tartarus, putting them into gloomy dungeons to be held for judgment" (2 Pet. 2:4).

Vincent comments, "It is strange to find Peter using this Pagan term, which represents the Greek hell, though treated here as not equivalent to Gehenna, but as the place of detention until the judgment."[5]

In contrast, Paradise is a word of Persian origin, and means "garden." Persian kings and nobles used to surround their homes with great parks, stocked with beautiful trees and shrubs, populated by animals, both wild and tame. Pember notes: "Some suppose these parks to have been reminiscences of a tradition of Eden: at any rate a place of this sort was called a paradise."[6]

The connection with Eden can be seen in John's statement that the tree of life is there. While the point may be taken symbolically, nevertheless the identification is significant. In Christ,

---

5. Marvin Richardson Vincent, *Vincent's Word Studies in the New Testament*, Vol. I (McLean: MacDonald Publishing Co., 1886), 691.

6. G. H. Pember, *Earth's Earliest Ages* (Grand Rapids: Kregel Publications, 1942), 109.

access to the tree of life is restored; we are returned to Eden. "He who has an ear, let him hear what the Spirit says to the churches. To him who overcomes, I will give the right to eat from the tree of life, which is in the paradise of God" (Rev. 2:7).

As a result of Christ's resurrection, Paradise has been moved (or it is possible that there were two Paradises—an earthly one, and a heavenly one). In the Older Testament, the saints of God expected to descend to Sheol; we now expect to ascend and be with Christ (2 Cor. 5:8). At any rate, our destination as Christians is not subterranean.

> I know a man in Christ who fourteen years ago was caught up to the third heaven. Whether it was in the body or out of the body I do not know—God knows. And I know that this man—whether in the body or apart from the body I do not know, but God knows—was caught up to Paradise. He heard inexpressible things, things that man is not permitted to tell. (2 Cor. 12:2–4)

Paul wrote this after the resurrection, so Paradise was now "up" and to be identified with the third heaven. The third heaven is quite an interesting idea. The ancient consensus was that there were seven heavens, corresponding to the seven planets. Some thought there were more, and others thought there were as few as three. Paul does not say which school he belonged to in this regard, but he is in agreement with the ancient identification of Paradise and the third heaven. This is the possible basis for Lewis's treatment of Perelandra. This concept of various levels in the heavens can be seen in Hebrews.

> Therefore, since we have a great high priest who has gone through the heavens, Jesus the Son of God, let us hold firmly to the faith we profess. (Heb. 4:14)

And of course, having ascended, Jesus is now at the right hand of the Father, far above all the heavens (Heb. 7:26).

Gehenna

Our word "Hell" does not originate in the classical languages—we see it both in Old English and Old Norse. In Norse, for example, Hel was the name of the goddess of the Underworld. Unfortunately, the English word "hell" is used to translate entirely different words in the original language of Scripture. When we use the word today, most understand it to refer to the final destination of the damned, after the Last Judgement.

The Greek word for this final hell is "Gehenna," which comes from the Valley of Ben Hinnom. This valley had been the place where Molech was worshipped, and where the Israelites caused their children to "pass through the fire." That is, they sacrificed their children there.

> "The people of Judah have done evil in my eyes," declares the Lord. "They have set up their detestable idols in the house that bears my Name and have defiled it. They have built the high places of Topheth in the Valley of Ben Hinnom to burn their sons and daughters in the fire—something I did not command, nor did it enter my mind. So beware, the days are coming," declares the Lord, "when people will no longer call it Topheth or the Valley of Ben Hinnom, but the Valley of Slaughter, for they will bury the dead in Topheth until there is no more room." (Jer. 7:30–32)

Later on, the godly king Josiah defiled the pagan places of worship so they could be used no longer, and the place became a garbage dump, with fires burning there all the time. Because of its awful history, and because of how it looked in the present, the name was applied to the place of final judgment.

Who is in danger of going to this awful place? Jesus says that the fire of this hell is for those who call their brother "fool" (Mt. 5:22), those who did not take sin seriously (Mt. 5:29–30; 18:9; Mk. 9:43–45), those who listen to hypocritical false teachers (Mt. 23:15), those who praise a godly past while opposing godliness in the present (Mt. 23:29–36) and those who refuse to help Christ by refusing to help those in need (Mt. 25:41–46). James instructs us that we must be on guard; hellfire can spread to the tongue, and be spread by it (Jas. 3:6).

Jesus tells us that we must fear, not man, but rather the One who controls whether or not we go to this place (Mt. 10:28; Lk. 12:5).

As is obvious in these references, one of the ways the final judgment is described is by means of fire. It is a "hell of unquenchable fire," for example (Mark 9:43). Jesus takes some imagery from Isaiah's prophecy about the exclusion of the Jews from the promises (Is. 66:22–24), and applies it to the final state of the lost (Mk. 9:48). With either application, the picture is sufficiently horrifying. The worm does not die, and the fire does not go out.

This final state of the lost is described in the Book of Revelation as a lake of burning fiery sulfur (Rev. 19:20; 20:10; 21:8). The torment of this second death is described as everlasting. The imagery is possibly taken from the destruction that befell the Cities of the Plain in the book of Genesis (Gen. 19:23–24).

Fire is not the only image for the final judgment, however. There is also the frightening prospect of eternal blackness and darkness. Both Peter and Jude describe the destiny of false teachers this way. "They are wild waves of the sea, foaming up their shame; wandering stars, for whom blackest darkness has been reserved forever" (Jude 13).

Peter says the same: "These men are springs without water and mists driven by a storm. Blackest darkness is reserved for them" (2 Pet. 2:17).

Jesus uses the picture of darkness as well. He says: "But the subjects of the kingdom will be thrown outside, into the darkness, where there will be weeping and gnashing of teeth" (Mt. 8:12).

At the last judgment, Hades will be emptied (Rev. 20:30). The dead will be raised, both the godly and ungodly (Jn. 5:28–29). They will all, small and great, be judged for what they have done (Rev. 20:30). As a result of the judgment, death and Hades both will be thrown into the lake of fire (Rev. 20:14) This shows the clear distinction between Hades, which is the temporary abode of the dead, and Hell, which is the final abode of the damned. The only escape from either is to have your name in the Book of Life (Rev. 20:15).

According to angelic census, laid
Before the bounds for nations were
Established by the One who nations made,
Those nations drew their numbered lot.

But now the ruling principalities
Behold their realms begin to shake
And try to keep the gain from such as these
Who preach with all the zeal of men.

The archon falls and from that place retreats
(The place where he received his wound),
And from that lower vantage he defeats
All those who listen to his words.

He lies . . . the lying does him little good
Beneath the wielded iron rod.
All blinded effort vain; he never could
Withstand this nation's sovereignty.

Incoming days the God of peace will crush
That ancient seraph underfoot,
And then will all the frantic demons rush
Into the black, reserved pit.

2

CELESTIALS & THRONOPHANIES

Terry Morin

There is a class of life within God's creation whose history and destiny parallels that of the human race in several respects. Some members of this class were present in Eden after our parents' fall, and some fell from their own first estate. Some will join redeemed and glorified humanity before the throne of God, and some will join the devil in the lake of fire. They are the celestials, otherwise known as the seraphs, cherubs, and living beings generally associated with the presence of God and pictured in the thronophanies[1] of Isaiah, Ezekiel, and St. John. These celestial ones are neither chubby, naked infants nor lithe, effeminate wall-flowers,[2] but are fearsome, majestic, winged creatures, clothed in fire and speaking in thunder.

God's revelation of these creatures includes both cautions and encouragements to those who would attempt to survey the mighty race. The metaphor of a survey is a fit one for the study of this topic, and for this essay. As we shall see, the biblical data enables one to study the celestials from a safe distance, but does not give one leave to mingle informally. It is the purpose here to collect and correlate

1. The word is a compound of the two Greek words, *thronos*, and *phaino*, meaning "throne," and "appearing," respectively.
2. These are only two of the reported caricatures of angelic beings. In the author's preface to *The Screwtape Letters*, C. S. Lewis comments on the attempts of Raphael, Dante, Milton, and Goethe to give description to angels and cherubs.

the biblical data, to answer questions which are answerable from the texts, and to define the bounds of those which are not.

One could argue, and with considerable evidence from history, that the "hidden agenda" is the exegete's equivalent to the sandals of Moses. They are forbidden on holy ground. The presence of this contraband pollutes the scholar's study as easily as the archeologist's diggings. Theological systems have all kinds of intended and unintended consequences, some of them contrary to the biblical teaching. The clear and present danger of commitment to a system is that the clear teaching of the text may be set aside.

Just as with every text there is a context, so with every context there is a worldview. Actually, in any context there are several worldviews, the prophet's, the hearer's, and the one progressively unveiled through the revelation, to which the first two must conform. Much of the labor of Bible study for the late twentieth-century believer is the reconstruction of those first two worldviews, in order that the revelation may be more fully understood. Unfortunately for many today however, the reconstruction of the prophet's worldview is replaced by the imposition of the modern reader's worldview. The consequences of this practice are easily seen in cosmology and are illustrated with the examples of the Gnostic,[3] the neo-orthodox, and the higher critic.

The Gnostic brings a dualistic worldview to the Bible. It is not, however, the biblical dualism of good and evil, but a dualism of spiritual and material. The spirit realm is good, and the material realm evil beyond redemption. The Gnostic would rewrite Habakkuk 1:13 to read, "You are of purer eyes than to behold matter, and cannot look on created beings." Accordingly, the throne room scenes represent impossible realities. The transcendent God could not actually have a throne surrounded by four created beings. The one on the throne is therefore not the transcendent God but the

3. The English word "gnostic" is a transliteration of the Greek word *gnosis*, meaning "knowledge."

umpty-umpth emanation of Him, and therefore, the throne room scenes tell us little or nothing about Him.

The neo-orthodox also brings a dualistic worldview to the Bible, but it is a distortion of the biblical one. The neo-orthodox correctly perceives the "otherness" or transcendence of God, while denying to Him genuine immanence. For him, God is "wholly other" and no genuine contact is possible. The Scriptures are not the word of God; they become God's word to each of us in personal, mind-numbing encounters which leave us or the prophets unable to relate their real content. What Isaiah saw in his vision of the heavenly palace did not have objective, observer-independent reality, but was only the emotional after-effect of an encounter with the Christ, and is therefore not suitable material for analysis and classification.

The practitioners of the historical-critical brand of exegesis have contributed very little to the church's understanding of the message of the texts of Scripture. Historically, use of this exegetical method has given us analysis of the literary form, textual history and variants, linguistic context of a text, indeed, everything except what the prophet meant to say. Instead of enabling the text to live and speak to men, they content themselves with producing a silent, dissected corpse. In their application of rules of scientific evidence to the Scriptures, they at once dismiss the miracles, visions and theophanies, and with them, any possibility for serious consideration of the celestial creatures.

These few examples are included as a reminder of how anti-biblical worldviews or views of revelation may emasculate the text and give theological or moral refuge to those who wish to evade its consequences.

In taking these cautions to heart one must remember that a caution is not a prohibition. There are, in fact, many encouragements to our study contained within the sacred texts themselves, and we would be wise to be encouraged thereby.

One which would appear to even a casual reader of the Bible is the frequency and distribution of references to angelic and celestial beings. References appear in thirty-two of the sixty-six books of the Bible. Of the seventeen Old Testament books containing such references, eleven are historical books. Fifteen of the New Testament books refer to angelic or celestial beings.

A second encouragement to the study of the celestials is the variety and detail of the descriptions given for these creatures. The variety almost defies one's powers of description and classification. The detail is selective, giving considerable data on some features and completely ignoring others.

Another reason for a serious study of these creatures is their close association with the presence of God. Seven times in the Old Testament the Lord of Hosts (*Yahweh Sabaoth*) is said to be "enthroned between the cherubim" (1 Sam. 4:4; 2 Sam. 6:2; 2 Kgs. 19:15; 1 Chr. 13:6; Ps. 80:1; 99:1; Is. 37:16). With a few minor exceptions, all appearances of the seraphim, cherubim, and living ones are as throne attendants.

The cherubim are most frequently mentioned in the Old Testament historical books, and are physically represented in the tabernacle of Moses and the temple of Solomon. The physical representations include the solid gold and gold-overlay cherubim overshadowing the mercy seat, as well as the carvings of cherubim on the walls, doors, and furniture of the Holy Place. The physical form of the cherubim was made known to Moses on Sinai (Exod. 25:40), and to David by the Spirit (1 Chr. 28:12, 19). The presence of cherubim is thus an important feature of both the earthly and heavenly tabernacle, and even though their exact form was forgotten by the time of Josephus,[4] there are sufficient references to attempt a partial description, to which we now turn.

---

4. Flavius Josephus, *Antiquities of the Jews* (Grand Rapids: Kregel Publications, 1960), viii, iii, 3.

The Relevant Texts

The purpose here is to collect in one place the varying descriptions and references to seraphim, cherubim, and living ones and then to compare, contrast, and correlate the biblical information (see Table 1).

The first explicit mention of cherubim occurs in the context of the expulsion of Adam and Eve from Eden, and is described in Genesis 3:22–24. In the opinion of several lexicographers, the etymology of "cherubim" is doubtful. If the word is of Phoenicio-Shemitic origin, then it may mean either "divine steed" or "one who is near to God."[5] The Akkadian cognate verb means "to bless, praise, adore."[6] Unverified connections to Assyrian winged bulls and Persian griffons exist in the literature.[7] Any one of the first three meanings is reflected in the biblical usage of the word.

The cherubim of Genesis 3, however, are stationed on the east side of Eden as guardians of an earthly location, effectively denying immortality to the fallen pair. No description of the cherubim is given by Moses, except to say that they were accompanied by a self-turning, flaming sword. By Moses' day the form of the cherubim was a matter of, at least, priestly knowledge. No further mention of the guardians is made in chapters 4–6 of Genesis, and one assumption is that the cherubim remained at the east of Eden until Noah's day as the meeting place of God with fallen men.

There are two exceptions to this possibility, the first being that wayward cherubim are included in the "sons of God" of Genesis 6:2, 6 or the wayward angels of Jude 6. The latter is highly

5. Wilhelm Gesenius, *Hebrew and Chaldee Lexicon to the Old Testament Scriptures*, trans. S. P. Tregelles, (Grand Rapids: Baker Book House, [1847] 1984), 413.

6. *Theological Wordbook of the Old Testament*, Vol. 1, ed. R. Laird Harris (Chicago: Moody Press, 1980), 454–455.

7. *Hebrew and English Lexicon of the Old Testament*, ed. F. Brown, S. R. Driver, and C. A. Briggs (Oxford: Clarendon Press, 1906), 500–501.

Table 1: Summary of the Biblical References to the Cherubim, Seraphim, Ophanim, and Living Ones

Passage	Location	Function	Description				Other
			Wings	Faces	Hands	Voice	
CHERUBIM							
Genesis 3:24	Eden	Guardian					Accompanied w/flaming sword
Exodus 25	Tabernacle		Yes	Yes			Over the mercy seat
1 Chronicles 28	Temple		Yes	Yes			Called "the chariot"
Psalm 18:10	Heavens	Steed					Associated w/wind
Psalm 80:1	Throne	Attendants					
Psalm 99:1	Throne	Attendants					
Ezekiel 10	Temple	Escort	Four	Four	Yes		Full of eyes
Ezekiel 28	Eden	Covering					Associated w/King of Tyre
Ezekiel 41	Temple			Two			Carved between palm trees
Hebrews 9:5	Tabernacle	Covering					Cherubim of glory
SERAPHIM							
Isaiah 6:2, 6	Heavens	Attendant	Six	Yes		Yes	Thunder; burning appearance
OPHANIM							
Ezekiel 1, 10	w/Cherubim						Awesome height; full of eyes
LIVING ONES							
Ezekiel 1	Whirlwind	Throne	Four	Four	Yes		Associated w/Ophanim
Ezekiel 10	(see Cherubim)						
Revelation 4–6, 15, 19	Heavens	Attendant	Six	Four		Yes	Thunder; full of eyes

speculative as there is no indication that cherubim would ever be classed with angels. With the desertion of their appointed post as guardians of the garden and commingling with the daughters of men, a realistic option would be the destruction of both the garden and the cherubim's temptation.

The second, and less speculative, exception is that the anointed cherub of Ezekiel 28, incarnate in the King of Tyre, was at one time a guardian cherub in Eden. Ezekiel testifies both to the Edenic sojourn and subsequent fall of the cherub (Ezek. 28:11–19).

The next appearance of cherubim occurs on the Mount of God, Sinai, in the vision given Moses of the heavenly tabernacle. This was the pattern shown to him on the mountain, from which the plans for the earthly copy were made. One could not have constructed the solid gold images from the description given in Exodus 25, and one must again assume that the shape was of common knowledge, or at least to Moses, Bezaleel, and their helpers. The number of wings and faces is not given, though the two cherubs are said to face the mercy seat, and their wings are said to be outstretched over, and covering, the ark of the covenant. In addition, God states that He will speak from between the golden replicas (Exod. 25:22).

The two cherubs of Solomon's temple were apparently identical in form, albeit larger in size, to those of the Mosaic tabernacle. In addition to the gold-covered cherubim overshadowing the ark of the covenant, cherubim were carved on the walls and furnishings of the temple. An interesting reference in 1 Chronicles 28:18 identifies the gold cherubim with outstretched wings as "the chariot." "And by weight he gave gold . . . for the altar of incense, and for the construction of the chariot, that is, the gold cherubim."

A curious parallel to this reference is found in 2 Kings 2:12, in which the assumption of Elijah is recorded. As Elisha watches, a whirlwind carrying a fiery chariot takes his master and disappears into heaven. Elisha exclaims, "My father, my father, the chariot of Israel and its horsemen." The association of the cherubim, a chariot, and a whirlwind is also encountered in passages yet to be discussed.

In at least three places the psalmist refers to cherubim, and two of the references allude to the enthronement of God between the cherubim (80:1; 99:1).[8] The allusion is an obvious one in light of the frequent manifestation of the glory of the LORD above and between the golden cherubs of the most holy place.

The first reference, however, is Psalm 18:10, and pictures the Deliverer of David as riding on a cherub. A single cherub is here described as the royal mount, in contrast to the cherubim, which have been described as the chariot.

Other than an incidental reference in Isaiah 37:16,[9] the next reference to cherubim is found in the prophecy of Ezekiel and his vision of the departing Shekinah. Actually, there are three separate references, the last two being 28:11–19 and 41:18–25. The cherub of chapter 28 is identified as the King of Tyre. He was an anointed cherub, and one who covers or overshadows, a possible allusion to the overshadowing cherubs of the temple. The cherub was present in Eden, and also on the holy mountain of God, a reference either to Eden or to a heavenly mount of assembly. Ezekiel describes the cherub's fall, his expulsion from the holy mount, and his eventual humiliation and destruction. The covering for the cherub included nine types of precious and semi-precious stones set in gold.[10] The prophet also notes that timbrels and pipes were prepared for this cherub on the day of his creation, indicating a musical function or activity.

This passage is essentially a eulogy for the fallen cherub, given in the context of the prophecy of the fall of Tyre. The cherub, who

8. Five other references to the same are 1 Samuel 4:4; 2 Samuel 6:12; 2 Kings 19:15; 1 Chronicles 13:6; and Isaiah 37:16.

9. This is a cross-reference to 2 Kings 19:15, the prayer of Hezekiah.

10. The nine stones are identical to those of the first, second, and fourth row on Aaron's breastplate (Exod. 28:17–20).

once overshadowed the kingdom of Tyre and reigned incarnate as king, fell from the holy mountain, lost the kingdom and was himself destroyed.

The later mention of cherubim in chapter 41 indicates that in the new temple of Ezekiel's vision cherubim were carved on the walls and doors of the inner sanctuary. There is no mention of golden images of cherubim in the temple of Ezekiel's vision. The first passage in which the prophet directly refers to cherubim is chapter 10. The prophet has just seen a vision of the divinely appointed destruction of the city of Jerusalem and of the temple. In chapter 10 he records a vision of the theophanic glory cloud leaving the temple. Under the glory cloud, or shekinah, are four cherubim and four ophanim. The cherubim have four wings, four faces/ heads, have hands under the wings, and are covered with eyes. The faces are identified as those of a cherub, man, lion, and eagle. The wheels, or ophanim, are covered with eyes, are said to be indwelt by the spirit of the cherubim, and move in exactly the same way as do the cherubim. In Daniel's vision of the Ancient of Days there is mention of a wheeled, fiery throne (Dan. 7:9–10). There is apparently an altar or burner in the midst of the cherubim, as the divine destroyer is commanded to take coals from among the cherubim to scatter over the city. The cherubim take coals in a hand and give them to the divine destroyer. Mediation of the wrath and judgement of God is apparently one role of the cherubim associated with the theophanic glory cloud.

Aside from the physical description of the cherubim, this passage is an important one in that twice the prophet notes that these cherubim are one and the same as the living creatures of Ezekiel 1. The living creatures or cherubim of Ezekiel 1 make their entrance in a whirlwind from the north. The whirlwind comes with a raging fire in its midst and is accompanied by the glory cloud and an occupied throne. The four cherubim have the likeness of a man, four faces/heads, four wings, hands under the wings, straight legs, and the soles of their feet are like those of calves. The faces are identified as those of a man, lion, ox, and eagle. Their wings are outstretched and cover their bodies. The cherubim have the appearance of burning coals or torches, their motion is like that of lightning, lightning proceeds from them, and a fire rages in their midst. Like the cherubim of Ezekiel 10, these cherubim are accompanied by ophanim of awesome height, and full of eyes.

The two descriptions are essentially identical, with the exception of the identities of the faces. One list includes the face of a cherub, while the other includes that of an ox. One should also note that two of the faces, that of the eagle and the lion, belong to unclean animals. Calvin held that the cherubim were symbolic of the ultimate redemption of the whole creation. He understood the faces to be representative of all land-based life. His opinion has some support in that the number four is often used in association with earthly affairs, for example, the four winds, the four corners of the earth.[11] Others have speculated that the cherubim were symbolic of redeemed humanity, the fullness of the Deity, of the angelic nature, or of the Divine manhood of Jesus Christ.[12]

The visions of Ezekiel provide the clearest description of the cherubim. They are fiery, four-winged creatures usually identified with the glorious throne-chariot of God. With the exception of a brief mention in Hebrews 9:5, the visions of Ezekiel are also the last direct references to cherubim in the canon of Scripture.

The only mention of the seraphim is found in the sixth chapter of Isaiah, a record of a vision of the prophet in the year of King Uzziah's death. King Uzziah, monarch of the southern kingdom, was also known as Azariah, and was the leper king of Judah. He was striken with uncleanness after offering incense before the altar

---

11. John Calvin, *Commentaries on the First Twenty Chapters of the Book of the Prophet Ezekiel*, Vol. 1 (Grand Rapids: Baker Book House, 1979), 334f.

12. *The Pulpit Commentary*, Vol. 1, eds. H. D. M. Spence-Jones and Joseph S. Exell (Grand Rapids: Wm. B. Eerdmans Publishing Co., 1978), 74.

of incense in the holy place. He spent his days as the leper king in seclusion, and his son Jotham reigned in his place. Isaiah's confession of uncleanness should be understood in this context. Isaiah's vision pre-dates those of Ezekiel.

The etymology of "seraphim" is far less doubtful than that of cherubim. The root word is "burning," and "seraphim" may be read as "burning ones," or as "fiery serpents." The first reading is favored by modern lexicons,[13] and the second reading is favored by some older works.[14] There is also some evidence that Egyptian guardian griffons were referred to as "serrefs."[15]

An alternative etymology which reads "seraphim" as "burning ones" is suggested in the extra-canonical book of Third Enoch.[16] The seraphim are said to burn daily the accusations of the Adversary in the altar before the throne. The ascription "burning one" refers to the function rather than the appearance of the seraphim.

The seraphim of Isaiah's vision appear, not with a theophanic glory-cloud, but in a throne room scene. The throne is occupied and the train of the occupant's robes of state fills the throne room. The seraphs are in flight, using two of their six wings to fly. The remaining four wings cover faces and feet. They are of a burning appearance, and as they chant the Trisagion, their thunderous voices shake the threshold and door posts at which Isaiah lies prostrate. They respond to the enthroned One without evidence of a spoken command, and one seraph serves to mediate cleansing to Isaiah.

The only New Testament book to include references to celestials is the Revelation of St. John the apostle. In chapter four the apostle describes his vision of the heavenly throne room. The

---

13. Harris, *Theological Wordbook*, 884.

14. Gesenius, *Hebrew and Chaldee Lexicon*, 796.

15. Brown, *Hebrew and English Lexicon*, 977.

16. *The Old Testament Pseudepigrapha*, ed. James H. Charlesworth (Garden City: Doubleday and Co., 1983), 3 Enoch 26:12.

one who is seated upon the throne appears to be the same as in Ezekiel's vision. In the midst of, and around, the throne are four living creatures. Each of the four is six-winged, fully covered with eyes, and unceasingly chant the Trisagion. Each is identified with a single likeness, that of a calf, man, lion, or flying eagle. From the throne are said to come lightnings, thunderings, and voices, perhaps from the living ones.

In contrast to the throne-chariot, there are twenty-four thrones around the rainbow throne of John's vision, each occupied by a crowned elder dressed in white. The living ones lead both the elders (4:9–11) and the congregation of saints and angels (19:5) in antiphonal psalming. They also join the elders in taking harps and bowls of incense before the throne for the singing of the "new song" of 5:9–10. This song is likely an antiphonal one, with the living ones leading and the elders responding. The following structure has been suggested by Chilton.[17]

> *Living ones:* Thou art worthy to take the scroll and to break its seals;
> *Elders:* For Thou wast slain, and have redeemed us to God by Thy blood out of every tribe and tongue and people and nation;
> *Living ones:* And have made them kings and priests to our God, and they shall reign upon the earth.

The antiphonal structure is suggested by the change in the pronouns from "us" to "them," and is a simpler explanation than to include the living ones in the company of the redeemed.

The four creatures speak with voices of thunder, like the seraphim, call forth the four horsemen of chapter 6, and give the seven bowls of the wrath of God to the seven spirits who stand before the throne. Like the cherubim of Ezekiel, these living ones mediate the wrath of God on an unfaithful people and a defiled temple.

---

17. David Chilton, *The Days of Vengeance* (Tyler: Dominion Press, 1987), 179.

One should also note that no cherubim, seraphim, or ophanim are named in the apostle's record. The apostle, a relative of the high-priest, does not refer to the living ones as the cherubim. With these passages in the Revelation of John, the biblical record of the celestials closes, as must the discussion.

Summary

The purpose of this summary is to state what may be said of the seraphim, cherubim, ophanim, and living ones, and to attempt to rationalize the variety of the thronophanies.

Although there are indications of a hierarchical structure in the creation in general, there is no clear evidence of such in the class of celestials. There are distinctions, however, in the stations assigned the various creatures. The primary distinction appears to be between those creatures assigned to the throne room of heaven, and those which accompany the throne-chariot. The seraphim of Isaiah 6 and the living ones of Revelation 4 appear in the throne room of heaven, though not necessarily always at the same time. The cherubim and ophanim of Ezekiel appear with the glory-cloud and throne-chariot. It is also the cherubim who are reserved for earthly missions. (Note Table 2.)

The proposed distinction is not without objections. First, one may say that this multiplication of thrones has been made on insufficient evidence. In response, the scriptures speak of several other thrones, as for example, in Daniel's vision of the Ancient of Days (Dan. 7:9–10). As Daniel watches, thrones are put in place or set up. The throne of the Ancient of Days is wheeled and fiery, and accompanied by other thrones. In the Revelation of John, the apostle records a great white throne standing in solitary grandeur (Rev. 20:11). So the scriptures speak of different thrones, all occupied by the same Person, and a distinction between a throne-chariot and a throne in the heavenly palace is not an unbiblical one. Indeed, some sort of distinction is required by the biblical

Table 2: Summary of the Stations and Functions of the Cherubim, Seraphim, Ophanim, and Living Ones

Celestial	Station	Functions	References
Cherubim	Throne chariot	Accompany the throne Mediate God's wrath Escort translated saints	Ezekiel 1, 10 Ezekiel 10 2 Kings 2:12
	Earth	Guardian of locations	Genesis 3:22–24
Seraphim	Heavenly throne	Chant Trisagion Mediate atonement	Isaiah 6
Ophanim	Throne chariot	Accompany cherubim	Ezekiel 1, 10 Daniel 7:9–10
Living Ones	Heavenly Throne	Mediate God's wrath Lead worship, praise Direct angelic activity Chant Trisagion	Revelation 15:7 Revelation 4:9–11; 5:9–10; 19:5 Revelation 6:1–8 Revelation 4:8

texts. The descriptions of the living ones of Revelation 4 and the living ones of Ezekiel 1are at such variance that any attempt to homogenize the two into one new creature can only be done, in the author's opinion, by claiming that the features described are either illusory or purely symbolic. In addition, if the living ones of Revelation 4 and the cherubim of Ezekiel 10 are one and the same, it is an observation which escaped the attention of the apostle.

Second, one may object that if the cherubim do not surround the heavenly throne of Revelation 4, what aspect of the heavenly tabernacle do they picture? It is clear from Exodus 25:40 and Hebrews 8–10 that the features of the earthly tabernacle and temple were shadows and copies of the heavenly one. The apostle John refers to just such a "temple of the tabernacle of the testimony in heaven" in chapters 15 and 16. To this it may be said that making a distinction between the two creatures does not thereby banish the cherubim from the heavenly palace.

Although every attempt has been made to give exhaustive coverage of the biblical references to the celestials, it should be clear that the canon gives far less detail than one might desire. Just as the silence of Scripture on the childhood of the Christ has left a biographical vacuum and provided a literary entrée for a variety of apocryphal works, so has its silence or ambiguity on this topic done. Though similar treatment of apocryphal and pseudepigraphal works would be a useful complement to this survey, this author is not sufficiently familiar with that literature to do so.

There remain unanswered and, indeed, unanswerable questions concerning these glorious and mysterious creatures. The unanswered, though answerable, ones are largely those related to issues of Hebrew grammar and word origin, disciplines in which this author is unskilled. The unanswerable questions are legion in number, greatly varied in kind, and will probably continue to stimulate the imagination and frustrate the scholarship of Bible students. This frustration, and the uncertainties on many other such issues, will pass and be forgotten on that day when, in the words of Job, "in my flesh I shall see God" (Job 19:26). In order that our scholarship not be burned with the wood, hay, and stubble, may our imaginations be disciplined by the Word of God.[18]

18. Acknowledgments: The author wishes to gratefully acknowledge Douglas Wilson for the use of Godspeed in collation of the biblical references. The library staff of New St. Andrews College was also of great assistance in making extra-biblical materials available to the author.

3

THE GOVERNING PRINCES

Evan Wilson

It takes a certain nerve to delineate governmental systems. Teaching anything from constitutional law to high school civics demands a detailed understanding of the formulae that stand in place to guide our nation.

Imagine the difficulty if a request to understand the system of some place like Burma were to be placed before you. The task is finite, and yet a long way off. There is a philosophy distinct from the one which formed your own home politic, and we suspect that in the Burmese citizen's experience the law is understood with just as much historic and processed subjectivism as we possess.

So it is with a certain amount of fear that I approach the halls of heaven as though they were in Burma, and hope to make out for my audience some vision of the gods of nations, their doings and their purpose.

The task is not without another fear. Unlike Burmese laws, the government of heaven rules all of us. That being so, the teaching of St. Jude on the subject of the Glorious Ones is not unhealthy for us to remember at this point. "But these men revile whatever they do not understand" (Jude 10).

J. R. R. Tolkien says it neatly: "The gods are after all gods, and it is a matter of some moment what stories are told of them."[1]

1. "On Fairy Stories," *Essays Presented to Charles Williams*, C. S. Lewis, ed. (Grand Rapids: Eerdmans, 1966), 56.

I trust that this essay will clear the vapors of some traditional misunderstandings, and will be a help in comprehending a monumental realm. We have before us the government of the universe. God Himself, not James Madison, built *this* hierarchy. I trust such a lofty endeavor does not discourage the interested with its presumption. The task is finite, if only because the beings studied are created.

It is, by very nature, ordered and quantifiable. No system of law, especially from a perfect source, could be anything else. Not only is the realm finite but our access to it is also. The God of gods has revealed windows to that realm, and those in a document of limited size.

Do not think for an instant that this realm is therein codified like the Bill of Rights. We do not have at our disposal a constitution of the heavenlies. Other than the character of God, I am not so sure that one exists. The Word of God is predominantly a history. We see in it the manifestations of the principalities and powers, as in their history they define for us their nature.

Prior to the Flood mankind was one in nationality and language (if Genesis 11:1 is retroactive). The wickedness of man had consequently direct and quick communication to all in this early world (Gen. 6:5). The culmination of this was the rise of the mighty men of old, the Nephilim, born in unholy union from celestial sons of God (Hebrew, *bene elohim*), and earthly women.

It could be suggested that God's response to this perversion was a continuation of His reason for casting Adam and Eve out of the Garden (Gen. 3:22). When He brought on the Flood, His desire was that His "Spirit would not contend with man forever for he is flesh" (Gen. 6:3).

After all had been destroyed (except eight persons), mankind, after a period of wandering toward the southwest from the mountains of Urartu, came back to the Plain of Shinar. The place was good for the raising of civilization and they proceeded to build a city and a tower. The morality of their actions is not recorded but their rationale is clear.

> Come, let us build ourselves a city, with a tower with its top in the heavens, and let us make a name for ourselves, lest we be scattered abroad upon the face of the whole earth. (Gen. 11:4)

As admirable as this thinking was, God had seen its results before. If successful, "nothing would be impossible for them." The founding of Babel and the subsequent confusion of speech, are the beginnings of the rule of the Princes over man.

The Table of Nations in Genesis 10 and 11 surround and center on the story of Babel. It was a geographic center as "from there the Lord scattered them abroad over the face of all the earth." In the Table we see a record of the descendants of the three sons of Noah, and some of the nations descended from them.

Do I expect to be trusted in saying that this moment is the advent of Princes over nations? If nations, then princes? No, the Scripture bears witness to this interpretation. In Deuteronomy 32:8 it says:

> When the Most High gave to the Nations their inheritance, when he separated the sons of men, he fixed the bounds of the peoples according to the number of the sons of God.[2]

---

2. Certain texts read "sons of Israel," which is difficult to compute no matter how it is read. If it means the 12 sons of Jacob, it does not match any sensible numbering of the nations. If it refers to the nation in total, it is equally far-fetched, unless one is merely addressing enough room being made for these between .xed bounds of the peoples. Looking at the Conquest, it seems they weren't adequately "fixed." Also, the time reference in this verse is around the time of Babel at which time neither the nation nor individual Israel existed. The LXX reads "angels of God."

The association of a select group of celestials with the various nations is witnessed in antiquity by the writers of the pseudepigraphal books of 1 and 3 Enoch. Their mystical tone and arguable accuracy notwithstanding, they still show that the connection was made.

First Enoch is vague with a reference in 89:59 to "seventy shepherds" which is the traditional numbering of the nations from Genesis 10 (all the names minus Noah and his three sons), but 3 Enoch is more clear.

> Above them are seventy-two princes of kingdoms in the height, corresponding to the seventy-two nations of the world. (3 Enoch 17:8)[3]

> How many princes are there? There are seventy-two princes of kingdoms in the world, not counting the Prince of the World. (3 Enoch 30:2; see also 18:3)

In the rabbinic work *Pirke de-Rabbi Efiezer*, this clarifying quote occurs, "The Holy One, Blessed be He, descended with the seventy angels that surround the Throne of Glory, and they confounded their speech into seventy nations and seventy languages" (PRE 24).

This notion of the Sons of God as equivalent princes (versus the Sons of Israel reading) is in agreement with, though not confirmed by, God's remark at the time to some unknown plurality, "Come, let us go down, and there confuse their speech."

At this point the student of these things will be asking about for the purposes of God in assigning such angelic lordship. The

---

3. The LXX renders seventy-three, but eliminating the scribal error of the extra Cainan brings it to seventy-two. This also adds another argument for the proof of that scribal error. See my article "Are the Biblical Chronologies Between Abraham and Adam Reliable?" in *No Stone Unturned* (Moscow: Canon Press, 1989).

choice to separate men was due to mankind's corporate ability and it was effective in creating the provincial strife we know to this day. Yet why the Princes?

It could be shunted aside by the structural of "God likes to delegate authority," but that must be obvious. It is delegated therefore He must have wanted to delegate. Are there any reasons given in scripture? Yes, and in a very non-mystical passage, to be sure. The Apostle Paul, speaking to the Areopagites in the seventeenth chapter of Acts, verse 26 says, "And he made from one every nation of men to live on the face of the earth, having determined allotted periods and boundaries of their habitation, that they should seek God, in the hope that they might feel after him and find him."

This initial burden of spiritual guidance we now know to have gone somewhat astray. Not so much that Paul could not point to the altar to the Unknown God in Athens and say that in agreement with Epimenides the Cretan prophet that "we are indeed his offspring."[4]

The purposes of God at Babel were still operative on the hearts of men, but somehow not as fruitfully as might be hoped. The Princes had, by Paul's time, become enemies of God, as we will cover later. Some evidence for their failure is what we turn to next. In the Psalms the lament and accusation is clearest. In Psalm 58:1 we see David's concern:

> Do you indeed decree what is right, you gods? Do you judge the sons of men uprightly? Nay, in your hearts you devise wrongs: your hands deal out violence on earth.

4. See Acts 17:28. Epimenides was a religious teacher and wonder worker in the Greek world. There are varied dates for him. Plato puts him at 500 B.C. (*Laws* 1.642), while Aristotle places him at 600 B.C. (*Athenaion Politeia* 1, etc.). There was a rumor that he had an unusually long life span, with a sleep of some fifty years. He was a worshipper of the Cretan Zeus, and is referred to as a prophet by Paul in Titus 1:12.

Asaph takes up the thought in Psalm 82:1 with this clear statement:

> God has taken his place in the divine council; in the midst of the gods he holds judgment: "How long will you judge unjustly and show partiality to the wicked?"

Someone will point out that "gods" (*elohim*) in these passages can be rendered "mighty" or "judges" which, strictly speaking, is true. Still, I will defend my application on the authority of Christ, who when accused of claiming divinity quotes Psalm 82:6 in John 10:34:

> Is it not written in your law, "I said, you are gods"? If he called them gods to whom the word of God came (and Scripture can not be broken), do you say of him whom the Father consecrated and sent into the world, "You are blaspheming," because I said, "I am the Son of God"?

Christ makes it clear that it is *godhood* they are discussing. Given the word in the Psalm (the Greek word He uses is unequivocal; *theoi*, which is the plural of god) and given His divinity, He is not trying to water down the term and say "No, I am only like one of these men of ancient time, who for some unknown reason were called gods."

He was saying that if claims to divinity are blasphemy, then the psalmist was blaspheming in his extension of the concept to a whole council of beings, and wicked ones at that.

Our brief study has led us to this decay; the high spiritual council, the Sons of God, neglected their responsibility of guiding men to their Creator and in rebellion led them to wickedness.

Where had these fallen spirits led the sons of men? Across the globe, the nations of men were aware that they were being led. They worshiped these lesser gods, not as the Most High but as the one that their nation had most interest in appeasing. The kings of the countries many times considered themselves as the manifestation of the particular god/prince.

Pharaoh in Egypt was the epiphany of either Amon-Re, or the combination of the two.[5]

The Seleucid monarch, Antiochus IV was called Epiphanes, as he was the counterpart of Jupiter Capitolinus.

Followers of various gods fought bitterly to allow their god, false or true, the right to rule the nation. The names they had for them are as varied as the peoples—Zeus, Amon-Re, Ashur, Shamash, Enlil, Hadad-Rimmon (Zech. 12:11; 2 Kgs. 5:18), Tammuz (Ezek. 8:14) and Bel-Marduk (Is. 46:1; Jer. 51:44), to name but a few.

Some you will notice are biblical names. First of all, are the biblical references to the gods of these countries merely poetic, a symbol for the nation without real presence? Such a suggestion is only the fevered remark of an over-excited materialism. While it is true that wicked ancient man may invent a religion and god *ex nihilo*, it is also and equally true that modern man may with a false premise attempt to destroy the gods that exist from the hand of their Creator.

It is lawful to discount the fraudulent gods (Is. 37:19) which man has made, but it is not lawful to deny that which God has made (Exod. 22:28; Jude 8). Note Psalm 86:8: "There is none like thee among the gods, O Lord." Look at Psalm 138:2: "Before the gods I sing thy praise."

In the New Testament, we see St. Paul's remark, in the middle of a strong affirmation of the One God and the worthlessness of idols, that "there are many gods and many lords."

All this shows that the Bible bears witness to an assembly of gods. You will notice that each of these quotations are elevations

---

5. Under Akenaton, circa 1400 B.C., worship shifted to Aten the Sun Disk, but under his son, Tutankhamen, it went back to the orthodoxy.

of the true God, the Most High, or as the Scriptures have it, "the God of gods" (Ps. 136:2).

The biblical references bring us to these beings with the light on their true character and places them as any created being under the judgment of their God. "I will punish Bel in Babylon and take out of his mouth what he has swallowed" (Is. 51:44).

Bel is short for Bel-Marduk. Marduk was a storm god (like Zeus and Hadad-Rimmon) who, as told in the *Enuma Elis*, seized the High God position and became king of the gods. Bel means lord, in this case of Babylon. It is a variant of Baal which is the same, being the word for husband.

If ever there was well known misunderstanding it is over the Baalim. The lords so frequently mentioned throughout the Old Testament were not a monolithic whole, though they became unified as a type, the fertility god of the Canaanites, with time. They were not even by necessity evil, though they became synonymous with that also.

Even God Himself was referred to as a Baal (Jer. 31:32). Some were Lords of Cities (Baal Peor or Melquart the Sidonian Baal) others of moments (Baalberith: Lord of the Covenant), Tribes of Israel (Baal-Judah; called Kiriath-jearim later) or even of abilities (Baal-perazim: Lord of Breaches).

That in some of these cases the lord referred to may have been the true God and not some local authority is seen in the name Merib-baal, the son of Jonathan. Still the wicked varieties became so dominant that a godly usage of the term became impossible. Merib-baal's name, meaning "my lord is Baal" is changed to Mephibosheth, "dispeller of shame," and his uncle Ethbaal is changed to Ishbosheth.

Even God Himself reveals His unwillingness to be called by that usage, even in the husband sense (which in truth is not a different sense), in Hosea 2:16.

And in that day, says the LORD, you will call me "My husband," and no longer call me, "My Baal." For I will remove the names of the Baals from her mouth, and they shall be mentioned by name no more.

The Baalim are one of the most direct expressions of the rule of the heavenly beings over the nations of the past. Not all Baals are thereby princes. Many are simply lords over a stream, a hilltop, a grove of trees, or a piece of property. These would be considered nature gods like the satyrs, Pan especially, of classical religion.

The ones that concern us are those strong enough to rule a nation; the sky-baals, the storm gods, the sons of heaven. They had careers which, although unknown to us in most cases, spanned millennia. They took their people from city states to empires.

Matthew 12:24 broadens the career of the most famous of the baals—Baal-zebub, the god of Ekron, lord of the Swarming, prince of demons, the adversary, the Satan, the Prince of Rome.

Ekron was a city of the Philistines which stood directly west of Jerusalem about 25 miles distant. Elijah the Prophet rebukes Ahaziah, the King of Israel, in 2 Kings 1 for consulting this baal in his sickness and tells him "you will surely die."

This minor reference is only a moment in a long career but even before this moment we can see how he fits in the hierarchy which God had created. In Job, dating possibly before the founding of Ekron or the Philistine migrations[6] and in one of only three

6. The descent of the Philistines from Casluhim (Gen. 10), and their migration from Caphtor (Amos 9:7), is consistent with their in the Sea Peoples migrations in the twelfth century B.C. They do not become dominant in the biblical narrative until the judges of Israel started having conflict with the Five Lords of the Philistines, one of which was Ekron. Some consideration should be given to the possibility that Baalzebub's lordship (the Lord of the Swarming) was preference to the wholesale relocation of the Sea Peoples. The swarming of a colony of bees is the relocation of the hive.

Old Testament occurrences, it is shown to which body of celestials Satan belongs.

> Now there was a day when the sons of God (*bene elohim*) came to present themselves before the Lord, and Satan also came among them. (Job 1:6)

We have already covered how the nations were numbered according to the members of this august body and council and we can only surmise that the assignment given Satan sometime prior to the writing of 2 Kings was either, narrowly, Ekron, or broadly, Philistia.

This might also explain an aspect of the difficult passages on David's census. David's longtime war with Philistia could be the sense in which "Satan stood against Israel and incited David to number Israel" (1 Chr. 21:1; cf. 2 Sam. 24:1). Rather than the modern view of the tempter tempting we might have had the standing host of the Philistines inciting David to number his own host.[7]

Satan's adversarial role, from which he gets his two most popular titles,[8] in Job and the third and last reference in the Old Testament, Zechariah, is undoubtedly his heavenly chore in the assembly of the sons of God. It is not necessarily attached to his rule of a particular nation. When he falls from heaven, he falls from that position. "For the accuser of the brethren has been thrown down" (Rev. 12:10).

And the earthly kingdom, Rome? A good case can be made out of the Revelation. There, one can argue that he only controlled

---

7. The contradiction of God in one passage and Satan in the, other does not exist in the LXX, which has the Devil in both. If this is the correct reading, then God's seemingly unjust anger may have been an event which David's census preceded.

8. We never discover his name in the Bible, but the Satan means *adversary*, and Devil, the *accuser*.

the eight emperors from Augustus to Domitian (the seven-headed beast and the two-horned beast).

Even in his post-imprisonment debacle, he reaches for Gog and Magog, since Rome had long since perished.

The Pseudepigrapha notes a certain Samma'el as Prince of Rome but in Third Enoch 26:12, he is in concert with Satan in the accusation of the saints, and in 14:2 is the Prince of the Accusers. It shows that the dual responsibility is not an unknown concept.

Also some texts (Martyrdom and Ascension of Isaiah 2:2–6) just make Samma'el a name for Satan and even of Belial, the spirit of the unbeliever in 2 Corinthians 6:15.[9]

Other Old Testament princes get equal attention with Satan, and throughout Christian history some have been confused with Satan. This is due to a stripped down cosmology and the incipient dualism that demands some sort of archfiend to wage a timeless war with God until the end.

The idea given in Scripture is that Satan is merely one of the rebellious princes and sons of God and has more than likely completed his "allotted period" and fallen centuries ago to the judgments of God.

He gets a lot of New Testament coverage (while receiving virtually nothing in the Old) because a great moment in his "allowed period" coincided with the coming of Messias.

We will come back to him later, knowing the difficulty a modern Christian has in absorbing this kind of thinking, and also because his career is recorded to the end, in the end of Scripture.

Who are some of the other princes? Most obvious are the lords, unnamed, of Persia and Greece in Daniel 10:13–21. The

9. The connection of Rome with Ekron is tenuous. A speculation can be offered that since the Philistines were a part of the migrations of the Sea Peoples, their assigned prince may have been the same. Some of these, after sweeping past the Levant, fought a major sea battle with Ramses III on the Nile Delta in 1188 B.C. Defeated, the migration continued to the north coast of Africa and settled, according to the best guesses, in Sicily, Sardinia, and Italy.

messenger from God explains that the answer to Daniel's prayer was sent out three weeks earlier but he was prevented from delivering it by the Prince of Persia.[10] Michael "the chief prince" takes up the fight to allow the message to reach Daniel in Babylon. What does this tell us? For one thing, we see that God in His delegation of power and authority has subjected even His servants to the wicked resistance of the fallen. They can fight and restrain each other. God could certainly overrule the resistance, but He has chosen to allow them to sow their own reward or destruction.

It also seems that most of the princes have fallen. I don't mean the heavenly host but merely the princes of nations who seem to be a particular rank, and somewhat small number. The messenger to Daniel announces that he is going back to resume his fight against the Persian prince and will then fight the prince of Greece. As a side point he reveals that Michael is the only one who fights at his side in this heavenly contest. This may not mean personally alone, for in Revelation Michael is accompanied by an army in his war with the prince Satan.

They are not only leaders of mankind's nations but they also have a following in glory, not of other sons of God, but rather of angels and other celestials. It is also worthy of note that the messenger's personal war with these two particular princes corresponds with the rise and fall sequentially of both Persia and Greece. A hint to the identity of one, the prince of Greece, can be found in Revelation 9.

The armies of the Abyss, riding in punishment of mankind are led by their Prince, Apollyon. This period of the vision corresponds with the historic rise of the Greeks through Alexander the Great and his defeat of Persia and can be considered as a strong possibility when looking to mesh the various pieces of data.

---

10. Third Enoch names the Prince of Persia (Dubbi'el), and portrays him as an accuser of the saints in heaven.

The restraining duties of prince upon prince, which is reflected in the governments of earth, is also alluded in Revelation 9:14. "Release the four angels who are bound at the great river Euphrates" (in all likelihood, the Hellenistic kingdoms after Alexander). Also, earlier in verses 1–2, Apollyon himself is released from the Abyss to do what God had allowed.

There is a cryptic passage in 2 Thessalonians 2:6 which can be understood in this light. "And you know what is restraining him now so that he may be revealed in his time. For the mystery of lawlessness is already at work; only he who now restrains it will do so until he is out of the way." God's ability to enforce His "allotted periods" is manifest in these celestial wars and imprisonments.

Another of the Old Testament princes is the often abused Gog, the prince of Magog and Roash, chief prince of Meshech and Tubal. Magog, Meshech and Tubal are three of the seventy (or seventy-two) nations of Genesis 10.[11] Whoever they were, Ezekiel prophesies (in chapters 38 and 39) against this agent of those northern peoples (possibly the Scythians who as a horde were plundering the Fertile Crescent at this time).[12]

Gog has an undetailed but long history. His power, armies and short-lived assistance are called upon by Satan in his postmillennia (read, post-restraint) war on the "beloved city" in Revelation 20:7.

We must not forget Lucifer. Lucifer means the Light Bearer. In the only text with this name (Is. 14:12), the word is *heylel*, the Morning Star, or son of the Dawning. If a prince at all, this name would be consistent with the biblical and pagan association of gods

---

11. Roash is not Russia. Russia was founded by Vikings from Scandinavia. They were tribally known as Russ, and settled Russia 900 years after Christ.

12. These were nomadic peoples of the steppes between the Black and Caspian Seas, who were not unlike the Cimmerians they drove out. They reached their peak between 800 and 200 B.C., raiding everywhere from Europe to Egypt.

with stars. My question of the higher sense is only because Isaiah himself (51:44) equates the god Bel with Babylon and Venus the Morning Star is Inanna/Ishtar in Mesopotamian religion. It could be that it is a description of Bel-Marduk, but since Ishtar is the clear designate of the star named, and since Bel-Marduk's star is Jupiter, it is unlikely.

The only biblical association is, oddly, to Christ, who in Revelation 22:16, is referred to as the Morning Star (*orthrinos*; an epithet for Venus).

Perhaps we have multiple rulers over Babylon or merely a prophetic word to the presumptuous earthly king.[13]

The presumption itself is the most compelling reason to accept him as one of our princes. He says: "I will ascend to heaven; above the stars of God. I will set my throne on high; I will sit on the mount of assembly in the far north; I will ascend above the heights of the clouds, I will make myself like the Most High" (Is. 14:14).

These are not impossible thoughts for ancient kings, as many claimed deity, but this quote has a ring of more informed realms.

In the Testament of Solomon, the star of Beelseboul is the Evening Star, but that is the closest the two characters come. The Bible nowhere connects this prince with Baal-zebub. Only when unaware of the wide variety of princes, can an individual start blending evil spiritual forces into a convenient archfiend.

Another interesting aspect of this broad topic is, as is often the case, our tendency to make God, and in this case, the gods, in our own image. Certainly some of the celestial creatures do appear in human form and the sons of God enough so to perform the requirements of husbands in begetting children. But much of the Scripture's view of this world is different than that, what with cherubim, seraphim, chimera, satyrs and fire-breathing dragons. We, still in the grip of the anthropomorphic assumption, relegate those beings to a class dubbed "visionary" or "symbolic." In looking

---

13. Nabonidus, the last king of Neo-Babylon, in all likelihood.

at the princes we discover the monstrous is not set aside as we address this admittedly great body of real beings.

In Isaiah 51:9 it says: "Was it not thou that didst cut Rahab in pieces, that didst pierce the dragon?" Psalm 89:10 says: "Thou didst crush Rahab like a carcass, thou didst scatter thy enemies with thy mighty arm." This occurs in a psalm which five verses earlier asks:

> Let the heavens praise thy wonders, O Lord, Thy faithfulness in the assembly of the Holy ones! For who in the skies can be compared to the Lord? Who among the heavenly beings is like the Lord, a God feared in the council of the holy ones, great and terrible above all that are around about him?

Who is this dragon Rahab? The word for dragon is *tanniym*, meaning elongated monster. It is clear that this east is associated with Egypt, and its successes and failures were those of the nation. In a curse on Pharaoh, Ezekiel says for God:

> Behold, I am against you, Pharaoh king of Egypt, The great dragon that lies in the midst of your streams that says, "My Nile is my own: I made it" I will put hooks in your jaws.

Seemingly there is the understanding that a Leviathan-like serpent was the spiritual master/prince of Egypt. Leviathan himself is not known to have ruled a nation through his wicked ways (Is. 27:1), but his power is consistent with others who have.

His many-headedness (Ps. 74:14) is like that of the ancient serpent, Satan of Revelation, but it is most likely they are two similar beings, rather than identical.

It is hard to admit to reptilian celestials but even the seraphim (mentioned only in Isaiah 6) seem to have that form, that of flying serpents.

Some will object and say that the word is in reference to their shining, fiery quality. And when the word *seraph* is used of flying snakes (Is. 30:6) on this earth they would translate it "darting snake." This in spite of the fact that two of the most credible of ancient historians, Herodotus (Book 11.75) and Josephus (*Antiquities* ii.x.2), mention the existence of flying snakes in that same region.

We turn now to a biblical Prince who has no name we can assign. He is also in the monstrous class (to our perceptions), but his description is left undone because his class was from the cherubim. Since their qualities vary from cherub to cherub, it would be too much to presume in such a lofty task to describe this particular cherub's makeup.

Who was he? Remember the cherubim that God assigned to the guardianship of the Garden in Eden (Gen. 3:24)? It seems, from the witness of the Prophet Ezekiel that one of these, through pride in its adornment and splendor, fell to the realms of men and was allowed the rule of the Phoenician city/state of Tyre (Ezek. 28:11–19). He also has been traditionally confused with Satan with no available reason in the text.

Still needing mention is "the Prince of the Host" in Daniel 8:11. Subsequent verses suggest that it is God Himself but it is unclear whether the "Host" is an angelic army of God or the armies of Israel. Other defining references I have not yet unearthed, and the question is still unclear.

The last named biblical prince is Michael ("Who is like God"). Everyone knows him as an Archangel and lists him with others: Gabriel (a biblical favorite), Uriel and Raphael (occurring in the apocryphal Tobit and much of the Pseudepigrapha and making the four well known of the traditional seven).[14]

While it is true that in Jude he is referred to as an *archangelos*, it is in Daniel that his position as "chief prince" (10:13) is revealed. He is only "one of" which suggests either rankings between princes

---

14. The remaining three are traditionally named, without any spiritual authority, Raguel, Sariel, and Remuel.

or rank referential to human princes in his domain. The title of archangel favors the former interpretation.

Whom does he rule? Later in Chapter 10 of Daniel it calls him "your prince" but lest anyone think an individual like Daniel could have that great a personal guide let us look to chapter 12:7: "At that time shall arise Michael, the great prince that has charge of your people."

He has rule over Israel, but is clearly in greater submission to God than his brothers. He also rules with God over this stubborn people, as it says following the already mentioned passage of Deuteronomy 32:8 on the allotment of nations: "For the Lord's portion is his people, Jacob his allotted heritage" (v. 9).

Michael's position might be seen illustrated in type, if not actuality, in the angel whom Joshua discovers to be the "commander of the Lord's army" (Josh. 5:15). His role in other places is consistently martial. The title for Michael in Second Enoch 22:6 is *archistratig*, or high commander. This is the term used by the LXX in the Joshua passage.

Third Baruch 11:4, and many other places, render the word "commander in chief." Not all armies of heaven would be under him but those which protected Israel would be safe bets. Anything from the army of angels which Jacob sees at Mahanaim (Gen. 32:1–2), to the army of fire which Elisha saw encamped against the invading Syrians (2 Kgs. 6:17), to the cry "The chariots of Israel and its horsemen" (2 Kgs. 2:12; 13:14) could be moments of protective oversight under the aegis of Michael.[15]

The actions recorded of this mighty one are those which thrill the lovers of holiness. His challenge of Satan over the rights to

15. It might even be said that the armies seen in the skies prior to Jerusalem's destruction in A.D. 70 (mentioned by Tacitus) remind us of Michael. Tragically, if he and his forces were there, they stood by and rejoiced (Rev. 19:3) as the armies of the dragon destroyed God's beloved city, which had become the Whore of Babylon.

the body of Moses, and his respectful rebuke of that Glorious one (Assumption of Moses, which is quoted in Jude).

His rise for a time of trouble in Daniel is to an unspoken task, but by its timing in the chronology of each prophesy, is perhaps defined in purpose by the passage concerning him in the Revelation of John.

> Now a war arose in heaven, Michael and his angels fighting against the dragon; and the dragon and his angels fought, but they were defeated and there was no longer any place for them in heaven. (12:7–8)

It is amazing that down through church history, in a scene where two of the sons of God battle it out in a war to end an age, virtually everyone's interest is drawn by the prince who loses. It again inflates his status and ignores the victory of the Chief Prince, Michael.

Satan, the dragon, is merely another in a long line of powers that Michael and others have spent their obedient career restraining, subduing and defeating. It is also amazing that in the interests of inflating the archfiend they take his fall and place it before the world's beginning, while in the prophecy it happens just prior to the birth of the Messiah.

This, for the dragon, is his "allotted time." He raises his empire, Rome (the seven-headed beast which looks just like him), and goes about "seeking whom he may devour."

But in all cases, God ends this ancient system of celestial rule as He wills (Job 12:13–25). After the death of the second beast, the eighth emperor,[16] another angel seizes the dragon with impunity and locks him in the Abyss. It is said that he, during this

---

16. Domitian, who died in A.D. 96. If you count from Augustus, and discount the three failed applicants to the purple in the Year of the Four Emperors, the eighth is Domitian.

thousand years (hear in terms of the concept we have been addressing) "should deceive the nations no more."

How often we think of this fallen one as the personal tempter, and causal agent to every sin. Certainly he tempted the Christ. The one who had come to overthrow his temporary hold on mankind was come to earth. And what did he offer Jesus? The kingdoms of the world.

We usually think that this was his to offer through his hold on men through sin, but with this different understanding it was because he was providentially ordained by God Himself as an actual governing agent of the Roman Empire.

We know that "there is no authority except from God" (Rom. 13:1). Paul wrote this under evil emperors who were under an evil prince. And Paul cannot be accused of ignorance of this higher plane of authority. On the contrary, he seems to think it the primary area of concern.

> For we are not contending against flesh and blood, but against the principalities, against the powers, against the world rulers of this present darkness, against the spiritual host of wickedness in the heavenly places. (Eph. 6:12)

What could be clearer? He is even expanding our understanding by populating the realm with beings who are not in the modern Christian's glossary. He even grants godhood to this enemy in 2 Corinthians 4:4, but he also states that all these dominions and powers are by necessity subject to God because they were "created through him and for him" (Col. 1:16).

What other, since others were mentioned, can we know with biblical authority? The word "powers" is common enough but it shows up in Revelation 14:18 with "the angel who has power over fire." Interesting. It continues. Ephesians 2:2 says, "following the prince of the power of the air, the spirit who is now at work in the sons of disobedience."

This might mean Satan, but for any modern it would be healthier not to assign him a role where it has not been mentioned. We need a much broader vision of the heavenly contest. What is most interesting about these two spirits and their respective powers is that the areas of dominion happen to be two of the four elementals mentioned in Galatians 4:3–8.

> So with us; when we were children, we were slave to the elemental spirits of the universe . . . how can you turn back again to the weak and beggarly elemental spirits, whose slaves you want to be once more?"

The word is *stoicheion*, which in the philosophy of the age was the title denoting the elemental gods, Earth, Air, Fire, and Water.[17]

Between the two verses in Galatians it makes it clear that these are not "gods" by nature. Whether that is in reference to the princes who lord over those realms or merely the petty spirits, who were the rank and file of the "power," it still gives one pause in passages such as "the very stones would cry out" (Lk. 19:40).

Lastly, in the New Testament, we have the prince of demons. In Matthew, we come back to Beelzebul, the Satan, but it is best that we have broken the components of his history in this way.[18]

Without looking at the other princes, we hear "prince of demons" much like we hear "prince of Darkness," i.e., head bad-guy. It is our simple desire for a moral dualism—transferring to ethics what is actually defining a realm.

Christ makes this clear in His response to the seventy rejoicing that they could cast out demons. "I saw Satan fall like lightning from heaven. Behold, I have given you authority to tread upon

---

17. Empedocles 493–433 B.C. These basic elementals had something to do with the observance of special days, and other divisions of the calendar. This can be seen in the writings of some of the Greek philosophers.

18. In the Testament of Solomon 3, Beelzeboul is the prince of demons, and the tone eliminates any other standing.

serpents and scorpions, and over all the power of the enemy; and nothing shall hurt you."

Christ, in making the association, still manages to set aside the accomplishment, and says that other things are more important. Demons are nothing next to the greater concerns of the Christian. Christ remembers the more important moment when Michael cast Satan to the earth.

Personal salvation (Lk. 10:20), and the war with the princes, is the recommended field of battle. We have seen how St. Paul saw himself in primary conflict with the higher of the host, and in Acts 16:18 he shows the level of concern these lower beings deserve. To center on the mundane, even if it is metaphysically mundane, is to be dangerously blind to the tone of early Christianity.

Satan, it is clear from the synonymous use in Matthew 12:24, is also the prince of demons. We must say that, whoever these little irritants to sanity may be, their lord and prince was Satan. This is not necessarily different from his rule of Rome in that, as mentioned, the princes had heavenly dominion as well.

We know that in his fall Satan the dragon had an angelic army. Most tradition equates the demonic with his fallen comrades, but in sheer levels of glory (which don't seem to change with moral turpitude: see Jude and 2 Corinthians 11:14), they are miles apart. The demons could be from that host—but its more insignificant members.

Where does all this leave us? Satan, the last prince, was locked up for a thousand years, only to be released to make another frantic grab for revenge with his fellow prince Gog. He was then destroyed. Israel, since its destruction in A.D. 70, has left us without word from Michael.

Demons, if they are active, are left without a leader. And the nations of today—who knows if they have the high and mighty princes still guiding their fate?

It could be that a whole new set of more righteous agents, perhaps in the role of *archistratig*, have been set to the task. Those do not seem to command the fates of men as much as they command the armies of the Lord of Hosts.

Our impurities, as we see with Michael, do not flow uphill. Wicked princes turn men astray, not vice versa. What is sure in all this? The Christ said in Matthew 24:29 that "the powers of the heavens will be shaken," and in John 12:31 it says, "Now is the judgment of this world, now shall the ruler of this world be cast out."

St. Paul reveals that something in this world other than atonement for sin was accomplished on the Cross. "He disarmed the principalities and powers and made a public example of them, triumphing over them in him" (Col. 2:15).

This defeat is not necessarily coincident with destruction. God has always been God of gods and, as with men, is awaiting the proper time of judgment. The something new, like the new indwelling of the Spirit at Pentecost, is the Kingdom of God at hand.

The crashing of the stone on the feet of the statue of empires in Daniel was not merely the overthrow of the kingdoms of men, but the toppling of the princes. All the nations are now God's inheritance. All are His first generation rule. We are now, with new meaning at the end of this discussion, in the Kingdom of God and His Christ.

He has annexed the entire world to His kingdom. He no longer has merely the land of Israel, leaving the rest to the princes. The princes (those whom we have discussed, excepting the ones destroyed) may be wandering the heavens with their metaphysical forces, but Christ rules.

What Satan offered to give, Christ, knocking him down, took from him and received from the hand of His Father.

Luke 19:11–27 relates in the parable of the pounds how this coincides with rebellious humanity. The nobleman goes away to receive a kingdom and the unfaithful do not want His rule but their choice only affects their reward. He rules, He rewards the faithful, and His treatment of the rebellious is that of a king.

> But as for these enemies of mine, who did not want me to reign over them, bring them here and slay them before me. (Lk. 19:27)

> All authority in heaven and on earth has been given me. (Mt. 28:18)

Christ's apostles were to take the message of a new prince to the world. This prince will someday end the arrogance of mere men, who attempt to chart their own course. Today it is certain that it is He who sits enthroned on the Cherubim and rules with a rod of iron.

> As there be gods many, and lords many, but to us there is one God, the Father . . . and one Lord Jesus Christ. (1 Cor. 8:5–6)

4

DIVINATION & WITCHCRAFT

Greg Dickison

One of the purposes of these essays is to show the reader what God's creation contains beyond the visible realm. This essay takes a back-door approach, examining Scripture for the tracks left by certain aspects of the creation, rather than looking for positive declaratory evidence of their existence.

We live in an age when things supernatural are treated with great skepticism. In such matters, we have gotten used to rejecting certain beliefs as superstitious unless we have a clear revelation of their truth. This is not a bad practice, except that it can make us miss important things if we are overly cautious.

Cosmology is a good example. The Bible speaks of things which were perfectly clear to the original hearers because they understood the context. We have lost the context, and have no clear explanation of it. Because we don't understand it, and because of years of materialistic training, we reject it when it is explained. Thus we miss out on a lot of truth. My purpose here is to restore the context.

This essay is by necessity incomplete. Thousands upon thousands of volumes have been written on the this topic. Following all the little rabbit trails that lead off into related ideas would be the work of several lifetimes. If anyone wants to explore any area further, the footnoted works will be very helpful, and will themselves lead to myriad other sources.

General Background

Divination is man's attempt to foretell the future, or to discover hidden events by mystical or supernatural means. Another way of looking at it is that divination is, man's attempt to communicate with the gods. Many presuppositions underlie divination. One is that gods, or some spiritual beings, exist. Another is that those gods have control, or at least knowledge, of the events that make up and shape men's lives. A third is that men can find out from the gods the state of those events. Anyone who held these presuppositions would not begin any major undertaking without first divining whether conditions were favorable.

Divination was practiced by all the nations and cultures mentioned in the Bible, including the Israelites. Some forms of divination were approved by God, others were forbidden. In Deuteronomy 18:9–11, God warns the Israelites not to imitate certain practices of the Canaanite nations they are about to conquer:

> There shall not be found among you any one . . . that useth divination, or an observer of times, or an enchanter, or a witch, or a charmer, or a consulter with familiar spirits, or a wizard, or a necromancer.

The cursed nations had done these things and thus had made themselves an abomination to God. To save Israel from such a fate, God promised to send them a prophet like Moses, who would give them all of His commandments. They wouldn't have any need of the forbidden arts (Deut. 18:11–22). At some point, however, the people began to ignore God's command and follow the advice of those who communicated with the fallen spiritual realm. As a result, they were led away from worshipping God Most High.

One Hebrew word rendered "divination" is *khosem* (or *qosem*). It literally means "to divide," and is rendered "to determine by lot or divination."[1] Another word is *nachash*, which means literally

---

1. Robert Jamieson, A. R. Fausset, and David Brown, *A Commentary Critical, Experimental, and Practical on the Old and New Testaments* (Grand Rapids: William B. Eerdmans, 1976), 663.

"hiss" or "whisper," and is rendered to learn by prognostication, enchantment, or magic spell. The word is used in Genesis 30:27, when Laban says to Jacob, "I have learned by divination that the Lord has blessed me because of you." The KJV translates this as "learned by experience," which is a possible rendering. Another is that Laban had the grace and wisdom to discern by normal mental processes that his good fortune was due to Jacob's presence.[2] Divination can mean "to discern,"[3] but it is usually done by supernatural or magical means.

A further insight in to this statement made by Laban comes later in the same episode. Jacob gathers his family and goods together and steals away from Laban by night. Unknown to Jacob, Rachel has stolen Laban's household gods. When Laban catches up to them, he is very anxious to get the gods back (Gen. 31:19, 30). The word rendered "household gods" is *teraphim*.

Teraphim

The teraphim were images "used as objects of inferior worship, or for purposes of divination . . . and oracles"[4] and "as talismans for superstitious purposes."[5] It is possible that the teraphim were images used in some form of ancestor worship.

The word teraphim may be related to the Egyptian word *ter*, which means "a shape, type, transformation." *Ter* "is used in the Ritual, where the various transformations of the deceased in Hades are described."[6] A complete connection between the two words cannot be made. "The possible connection with the Egyptian religious magic is, however, not to be slighted, especially as it is not

2. Ibid., 206.
3. O. R. Gurney, "The Babylonians and Hittites" in *Oracles & Divination*, eds. Michael Loewe and Carmen Blacker (Boulder: Shambhala, 1981), 142.
4. Jamieson, *Commentary Critical*, 209.
5. Ibid., 210.
6. G. H. Pember, *Earth's Earliest Ages* (Grand Rapids: Kregel Publications, 1942), 164.

improbable that the household idolatry of the Hebrews was ancestral worship.[7]

Of course, the episode between Jacob and Laban took place before the Israelites had much contact with Egypt. But, given the common ancestry of man, it is probable that any connection between the two cultures came from an earlier common source.

Under the heading "Magic," *Smith's Bible Dictionary* has a good passage on the teraphim. Smith says that two other possible derivations of the word are "dancers" or "causers of dancing, "and "givers of pleasant life," referring either to nature worship or shamanistic magical rites.[8]

As to the divinatory nature of the teraphim, one commentator says they were "used at first merely as media in consulting God." Of Laban's images, he says, "those Teraphim were evidently not objects of worship in themselves; they were merely emblems or tokens, such as served pretty much the same purpose as pictures and images of the saints do amongst Roman Catholics of the present day."[9] Another says there is "no doubt . . . that the teraphim gave oracles."[10]

As to the mechanics of the teraphim, unnamed "Jewish writers" give this explanation: "being formed under certain constellations, according to the astrological notions of antiquity, they were made by the influence of magical art to speak at certain times in answer to questions."[11]

When all this information on the nature of teraphim is put together, it is not an unreasonable conclusion that Laban used his teraphim for purposes of divination, and that they were the means by which he discovered the blessing of Jacob's presence.

7. Ibid, 164.

8. William Smith, LL.D., *Smith's Bible Dictionary* (Old Tappan: Fleming H. Revell Company, 1982), 365.

9. Jamieson, *Commentary Critical*, 210.

10. J. R. Porter, "Ancient Israel," *Oracles*, 207.

11. Jamieson, *Commentary Critical*, 209.

Several explanations are offered for Rachel's theft. Since the teraphim could reveal hidden things to Laban, she had to take them to keep him from finding out Jacob's route of escape. Or they had value as fertility gods, and Rachel wanted to secure their favor in obtaining children.[12] According to Josephus, "the reason why Rachel took the images of the gods . . . was this, That in case they were pursued, and taken by her father, she might have recourse to these images, in order to obtain his pardon."[13] It is also possible that Rachel wanted to secure the divinatory benefits of the teraphim for her husband or herself.[14]

Teraphim are mentioned in several other passages. In Judges 17 and 18, Micah the Ephraimite makes a shrine with teraphim and installs one of his sons as priest. This was in the days when "there was no king in Israel; every man did what was right in his own eyes" (Judg. 17:6). The teraphim are an important item to the Danites on their journey to raid Laish. It is not made explicit that these teraphim were used for divination, but it is not unlikely. They were an integral part of Micah's house of gods, and it is possible they were the gods (or their representatives) for whom the house was built.

Judges 18:5–6 is enlightening. The Danites ask Micah's priest to "inquire of God" as to the success of their journey. The priest's answer, "though apparently promising, was delusive, and really as ambiguous as those of the heathen oracles."[15] The heathen oracles, as will be seen later, tended toward vague prophecies that could be called "fulfilled" with any number of outcomes, even

12. Ibid., 210.

13. Flavius Josephus, *Antiquities of the Jews*, Book 1, Ch. 19, Sec. 9.

14. It should be noted that in Genesis 35:2, 4, Jacob commands his household to put away their "strange gods." Presumably the teraphim were among them.

15. Jamieson, *Commentary Critical*, part 2, 117.

if the outcomes were mutually exclusive. God, however, was very specific in His pronouncements.[16]

We also know that God gave very strict instructions concerning His worship, and that inquiries were to be made by the Urim and Thummim. It seems unlikely he would answer to a Levite who was going about things in such a blatantly wrong manner. Nevertheless, the Danites were satisfied with the service, and took Micah's temple" with them.[17]

The Israelites were not the only nation to possess teraphim. In Ezekiel 21:21, Nebuchadnezzar, King of Babylon, stands at a fork in the road. In one direction is Rabbah of the Ammonites, and in the other is Jerusalem. He consults the teraphim to decide which city to attack first. "At his right hand was the divination for Jerusalem" (Ezek. 21:22). From this passage it is clear that the teraphim were used for purposes of divination.

The idols of the Babylonians were more to them than mere artistic renderings. Their idols were the very habitations of the spirits of the gods. Where the idol went, the god went too. When an idol was taken from a city, the god became a prisoner of the invading army, leaving the city without divine help.[18] It is possible that Laban, being of the same, yet more ancient, extraction as the Babylonians, had this view of his own teraphim, adding urgency to his desire for their return.

Teraphim are among the abominations that Josiah removed from Israel during his reign (2 Kgs. 23:24). They are lumped together with mediums and wizards, suggesting a connection with divination. The fact that they were abominations makes it clear that they were not being used as doorstops.

16. See, for example, 1 Chronicles 14:10, 14–15.

17. Note also that the legitimate house of God was standing in Shiloh this whole time (Judg. 18:31).

18. Donald A. Mackenzie, *Myths of Babylonia and Assyria* (London: Gresham Publishing Company, Ltd., n.d.), 61–62.

Testimony as to the snare the teraphim were to Israel is abundant. Zechariah 10:2 clearly shows that the teraphim were used for divination, and that they were a problem. They spoke lies which led the people astray. But they were not outside of God's control. Obviously, they were allowed to communicate with the people for a time, but in Hosea 3:4, their silence is foretold. God says He will remove all leadership and guidance from Israel for a time, so they will turn back to Him. The teraphim are among the forms of guidance removed.

Teraphim were present in David's house before he fled. In 1 Samuel 19:11–17, Michal uses teraphim to fool the guards while David escapes. There is no hint that these teraphim were used by David for divination, unless we imply guilt by association. But divination is never listed among David's sins. Michal's use in this passage appears to be purely physical: they were a handy diversion. It is possible they were put there by Saul. Nevertheless, there they were.

Belomancy

When the King of Babylon consults the teraphim in Ezekiel 21, he also "shakes the arrows." The practice of divination by arrows is called belomancy,[19] and was practiced extensively by the Chaldeans and the Arabs.[20] Various numbers of arrows with "answers" written on them were mixed in a quiver or laid out randomly. A question was asked, and an arrow was drawn to determine the proper course of action.[21]

The Tibetans also had a form of belomancy. Two arrows were stuck point down into a pile of barley. Around one arrow a white

19. The lxx uses the word "rhabdomancy," the casting of lots, which will be discussed more later.
20. Montague Summers, *The History of Witchcraft and Demonology* (Seacaucus: University Books, 1956), 182.
21. Ibid., 182–183.

cloth was tied, and a black cloth was tied around the other. These represented the fundamental positive and negative polarities in the universe. The inquirer then enters a kind of trance, and the arrows begin to move around in the barley. The movements are interpreted to find the answer to the question put to them.[22]

While the Tibetan method is more theatrical than that of the Chaldeans, both illustrate the influence of the gods. In Tibetan belomancy, the influence acts upon the arrows, the instruments of divination. But in Chaldean belomancy, the influence acts directly upon the person, not on the instrument. The god guided either the diviner's hand or the diviner's choice of arrow. I emphasize this point to show the implicit belief of the Chaldeans that the gods could influence the will and actions of the diviner.

Two other Old Testament passages concerning arrows need to be mentioned, if only to distinguish them. The first is in 1 Samuel 20. Jonathan shoots three arrows into a field to communicate to David Saul's intentions toward him. There is nothing here to suggest belomancy. There is no consultation, and no decision needs to be made. The arrows are merely a pretext which will allow Jonathan to rendezvous with David without arousing suspicion. There would be nothing unusual about a warrior going out to a field to practice his archery.

The second passage is more intriguing. In 2 Kings 13:14–19, Elisha first directs Joash to shoot an arrow to the east, declaring it "The Lord's arrow of victory . . . over Syria." Other than the mystic setting, there is nothing here to suggest the arrow was anything more than an illustration. Declarations of war were often made by a king or general shooting an arrow into an enemy's territory in a public and formal proclamation.[23] This was apparently Joash's purpose.

22. Lama Chime Radha, Rinpoche, "Tibet," *Oracles*, 14.
23. Jamieson, *Commentary Critical*, part 2, 403.

Next, Elisha has Joash strike the ground with arrows. The number of times Joash strikes the ground determines the number of times Israel will defeat Syria. Again, it appears that the arrows were symbolic of the strength of Israel and were an illustration of the prophesied defeat of Syria, but that there was no belomancy in the strict sense of the word.

Entrail Reading

The third method of divination employed by Nebuchadnezzar in Ezekiel was the looking at the liver. This divination was known as haruspicy, or extipicy. A question was asked and an animal sacrificed to the appropriate god. The god's answer to the question would be "written" in the configuration of the entrails of the sacrifice. Often multiple sacrifices were made; sometimes to make doubly sure of a correct interpretation, sometimes to make sure all the appropriate gods were consulted.

The ancients had haruspicy down to a science. Excavators have revealed numerous models of livers engraved with interpretive keys.

A "handbook" of entrail divination was found containing fifty-five tablets, complete with commentary.[24] The interpreter would carefully examine each organ for markings, check them in his guide, and write up an analysis of the omens, summarized at the end as to whether the signs were favorable or forbidding. In addition to the liver, the diviner checked the lungs, breastbone, stomach, vertebrae, spleen, pancreas, heart, kidneys, and intestines.[25]

It is possible that Balaam was practicing extipicy when he was summoned by Balak to curse the Israelites.[26] The story is found in Numbers 22 through 24. Balak sends his elders to Balaam "with

24. Gurney, *Oracles*, 148.
25. Ibid., 149.
26. Summers, *Witchcraft*, 174–176.

the fees of divination in their hand" (Num. 22:7), which makes it clear that Balaam was a diviner. He also had a good reputation. Balak tells him, "I know that he whom you bless is blessed, and he whom you curse is cursed" (Num. 22:6), and is willing to pay a very high price for his services. Balaam is escorted to the high places of Baal where he offers two sacrifices on each of seven altars, presumably to read their entrails. One historian believed that the seven altars were built for the Lords of the Seven Planets.[27] But whatever Balaam's purpose, he cannot contest with God, and blesses Israel in spite of Balak's insistence on a curse.

From the passage it appears that Balaam was not a true prophet of God, but a pagan soothsayer who was God's instrument. The Vulgate uses the term *harioles*, which is applied to a diviner of entrails.[28] Josephus gives a different perspective. He pictures Balaam as a great prophet of God who is acting the part of the obedient servant.[29] However, Balaam is slain by the Israelites when they make war on Midian, and in that passage he is expressly referred to as a diviner (Josh. 13:22).

It has been asked whether sacrifices in the temple could have any relationship to extipicy. The answer is clearly no. The sacrifices prescribed by God were all in the nature of offerings to God from the Israelites as a function of obedience, and not methods of determining God's will by reading entrails. Among the methods God says He will use to communicate His will to His people, extipicy is never mentioned. Even the sacrifices of the pagan nations could be offertory in character, as something that would be pleasing to the gods.

---

27. Ibid., 176.
28. Ibid., 175–176.
29. Josephus, *Antiquities*, Book 4, Ch. 6.

Hydromancy

Another method of divination is mentioned in connection with the patriarch Joseph in Genesis 44. After he had been made Pharaoh's second in command over Egypt, his brothers came to him to buy food. After their second purchase, Joseph had his servants place his silver cup in one of the sacks. This cup was Joseph's divining cup (Gen. 44:5).

One commentator says of Joseph's divining cup:

> It is not likely that Joseph, a pious believer in the true God, would have addicted himself to this superstitious practice. But he might have availed himself of that popular notion to carry out the successful execution of his stratagem for the last decisive trial of his brethren.[30]

Another commentator has the opposite view:

> In the first place it cannot be for a moment supposed that Joseph's claim, which here he so publicly and so emphatically states, to be a diviner of no ordinary powers was a mere device for the occasion. From the prominence given to the cup in the story it is clear that his steward regarded it as a vessel of especial value and import, possessing mysterious properties.[31]

Whether Joseph actually practiced divination or not, he says that he divines with the cup, and his servants attest to it, also. He was at least familiar with the practice.

There are two possibilities as to how the cup was used. One required that magical inscriptions were engraved in the cup or written on the inside in ink. Water poured in the cup would dissolve the ink, and it would be drunk. The drinker would gain whatever benefit the inscriptions were supposed to confer.

30. Jamieson, *Commentary Critical,* part 1, 252.
31. Summers, *Witchcraft,* 184.

The more likely explanation is that the cup was used for hydromancy, or divination by water. "The seer, or in some cases the inquirer, by gazing fixedly into a pool or basin of still water will see therein reflected as in a mirror a picture of that which is sought to know."[32] In modern Egypt, the practice is known as the Magic Mirror. Water or ink are poured into a boy's hand, and answers to questions will be seen therein.

Hydromancy, and various like divinations, are widely known. Augustine says that King Numa of Rome used hydromancy, and that he learned it from the Persians. By this method the gods were consulted.

Another form made use of blood to consult the dead.[33] The Babylonians practiced lecanomancy, where oil would be poured into water or water into oil. The patterns formed by the oil would be interpreted.

The same thing could be done by substituting flour for the oil, which was called aleuromancy.[34] The Hittite method involved putting a snake into a basin of water and taking omens from its movements.[35] Forms of hydromancy were also known in Scandinavia, Tahiti, Hawaii, the Malay Peninsula, New Guinea, and among the Eskimos.[36] The reading of tea leaves falls into this category.

Dreams

Dreams are another form of divination. God forbade the Israelites to follow dreamers of dreams if they led Israel to other gods, but dreams from the true God were legitimate. Joseph's dreams were portents of the future, which were fulfilled when he was made governor of Egypt (Gen. 37:5, 9). When he was in Pharaoh's prison, he

32. Ibid., 184.
33. Augustine, *The City of God*, Book 7, Ch. 35.
34. Gurney, *Oracles*, 152.
35. Ibid., 156.
36. Summers, *Witchcraft*, 185.

was enabled by God to interpret the dreams of Pharaoh's baker and cupbearer, and later the dreams of Pharaoh himself (Gen. 40:5–23; 41:1–32). Many other passages show God communicating with people through dreams.

Dreams have historically been held in high regard as carrying omens, as shown by the great importance attached to them by the pagan nations. Recorded instances of gods appearing to sleepers are found among the Sumerians, Hittites, Assyrians, and Babylonians.[37] This list is by no means exclusive. Dreams also came in symbolic form. Rather than a god appearing and giving a direct message, a story would be enacted which required interpretation. Both types of dream are found in scripture.

Dream interpretation was a valuable skill, one which commanded high honor and position. Great books full of symbols were compiled so that the omens delivered in a dream could be deciphered.

The Egyptian wise men and magicians held the office for Pharaoh, but his dream in Genesis 41 was beyond even them. When Joseph gave the correct interpretation, he was "set over all the land of Egypt," next only to Pharaoh himself (Gen. 41:39–40).

We see the same thing happening in Daniel chapter 2. The "magicians, and the astrologers, and the sorcerers, and the Chaldeans," were all brought before Nebuchadnezzar, not only to interpret his dream, but to tell him what it had been (he was apparently very skeptical of their ability and their motives). Daniel was able to do both, and was made "ruler over the whole province of Babylon, and chief of the governors over all the wise men of Babylon" (Dan. 2:48).

This is a good place to make a note about the class of magicians and wise men. The *khartummim* were the magicians of Egypt and the *khakhamim* were the wise men.[38] They are the ones who

37. Gurney, *Oracles*, 143.
38. Pember, *Earliest Ages*, 157–158.

opposed Moses and Aaron before Pharaoh. Besides having the skill of interpreting dreams, they knew certain magical arts which allowed them to imitate the miracles performed by Moses. But, like the dream interpretation, the magic had its limits: God proved more powerful in each case. The same thing is seen in Daniel, with the exception that the classes are expanded to include *ashshaph*, the sorcerers, *gazrin*, the astrologers,[39] and the Chaldeans. These groups were a special class which had great learning and acted as advisers to the kings. No doubt, part of their duties included divination. Daniel was being taught all this wisdom under Nebuchadnezzar in Babylon.

Necromancy

Necromancy is another method of divination. The idea is to contact those who are on the other side of the veil. A vivid account of necromancy is given in 1 Samuel 28. King Saul was desperate because of the Philistines. God would not answer his inquiries, and Samuel was dead. As a last resort, Saul sought a medium who could bring Samuel up from Sheol to tell him what he wanted to know.

The KJV says Saul sought "a woman that hath a familiar spirit." The Hebrew word used for "familiar spirit" is *ôbh*. The word can signify either the departed spirit which is evoked, or the person who controls the departed spirit.[40] The word may have originally signified a skin bottle, and came to be used for a medium because of the effect the familiar spirit had on the person. The transition to meaning familiar spirit is exemplified by Job 32:18–19: "For I am full of words, the spirit of my belly constraineth me. Behold my belly is as wine which hath no vent; it is ready to burst like new bottles." From this passage the word appears "to have been used of those into whom an unclean spirit had entered, because demons,

39. Ibid., 161.
40. Summers, *Witchcraft*, 179.

when about to deliver oracular responses, caused the bodies of the possessed to grow tumid and inflated."[41] As to the relationship between the medium and the familiar spirit, "it seems likely that a connection with an ôbh is frequently, if not always, the result of a compact, whereby the spirit in return for its services enjoys the use of the medium's body."[42]

There is a distinction between divination through an ôbh and divination by an independent spirit. *Yidoni* is Hebrew for "those who have knowledge." The word *yidoni* "refers to supernatural beings who possessed a knowledge beyond the human, which the diviner could extract from them by his special arts."[43] Thus, those who consulted water, arrows, or entrails were dealing with *yidoni*. The ôbh, however, is something in the possession of the diviner.

Various explanations have been given for what took place at Endor, very few of them accepting the passage at face value. One explanation is that the woman was a ventriloquist. She simply faked the whole scenario to get Saul's money. But this does not explain how she saw through Saul's disguise, or how she could give the answer Samuel gives, not being privy to Saul's life.

One historian of witchcraft says the theory that it was done by trickery

> hardly seems possible. It is not likely that she would have run so grave a risk as the exercise, or pretended exercise, of magical arts must entail were she a mere charlatan; an accomplice of remarkably quick wit and invention would have been necessary to carry out the details of the plot; it is surely incredible that they should have ventured upon so uncompromising a denunciation of the kind and have foretold so evil an end to his house. In fact the whole tenor of the story conflicts with this explanation.[44]

41. Pember, *Earliest Ages*, 160.
42. Ibid., 160.
43. Porter, *Oracles*, 204.
44. Summers, *Witchcraft*, 179.

Other explanations meet with similar difficulties. The most insurmountable obstacle is the bald assertion of scripture that Samuel came up from Sheol.

Python

One interesting account of divination is found in the New Testament. In Acts 16, Paul and his companions encounter a slave girl "possessed with a spirit of Python . . . which brought her masters much gain by soothsaying." The Greek word is *Puthon*, which "in Greek mythology was the name of the Pythian serpent or dragon, dwelling in Pytho, at the foot of mount Parnassus, guarding the oracle of Delphi, and slain by Apollo. Thence the name was transferred to Apollo himself. Later the word was applied to diviners or soothsayers, regarded as inspired by Apollo."[45]

Some light is shed on the spirit possessing this girl if we look at one episode In particular concerning the Delphic oracle. Herodotus relates the story of how King Croesus of Lydia made a test of the oracles to see which, if any, were true. He sent messengers to different oracles, and each of them was instructed to go to a particular oracle all on the same day and at the same hour. They were to ask the oracle what Croesus was doing at that moment. The Delphic oracle gave the correct answer, and Croesus made the oracle his counselor.[46]

According to the history of the Delphic oracle, it was discovered when a shepherd noticed his flocks go into fits when they approached a cleft in a rock. The shepherd decided to explore further and went near the cleft himself. Fumes were coming out of the cleft which overcame him, too, and he prophesied. The people supposed

45. John R. Kohlenberger III, ed., *The Expanded Vine's Expository Dictionary of New Testament Words* (Minneapolis: Bethany House Publishers, 1984), 320.
46. Herodotus, *History*, Book 1, Chs. 47–50.

these prophecies to be from a friendly deity, and they built the temple at Delphi.[47] Several deities were said to have made their home there, Apollo being the last and most famous. The oracles would only come one day during the year. On that day, the priestess would be taken into the sanctuary and placed on a tripod over the cleft, where she would be held by the priests.

As soon as she began to be agitated by the divine Exhalation, you might have seen her Hair stand on end, her Mien grow wild as ghastly, her Mouth begin to foam, and her whole Body suddenly seiz'd with violent trembling. In this plight she attempted to get away from the prophets, who were holding her as it had been by force, while her Shrieks and Howlings made the whole temple resound, and fill'd the By-standers with a sacred Horrour. In fine, being no longer able to resist the Impulse of the God, she gave herself up to him.[48]

After muttering the prophecies, she was taken down from the temple to recover. Frequently, however, the priestesses died soon after the ordeal.

Virgil draws a rather grotesque picture of this possession in Book VI of the *Aeneid*. The Sibyl changed "countenance and color" as the god drew near. Her hair was "tossed loose, and her heart was heaving, her bosom swollen with frenzy; she seemed taller, her voice not human at all. . . . More than her speech, her silence made the Trojans cold with terror." Aeneas prayed fervently to the approaching god. "But the priestess, not yet subject to Apollo, went reeling through the cavern, wild and storming to throw the god, who presses, like a rider with bit and bridle and weight, tames her wild spirit: shapes her to his control."[49]

47. Abbè Antoine Banier, *The Mythology and Fables of the Ancients Explained from History*, Vol. 1 (New York: Garland Publishing, 1976), 335.

48. Ibid., 339.

49. Rolfe Humphries, trans., *The Aeneid of Virgil* (New York: Charles Scribner's Sons, 1954), 145–146.

Notice how these two accounts of the priestess of Apollo are similar to the account of what happens to a medium in possession of a familiar spirit. There is also a similarity to the New Testament accounts of demon possession.

The slave girl Paul encountered was probably not a priestess of Apollo or of the temple at Delphi. As we have seen, the historical accounts of the priestesses were definitely not of girls walking the streets. But its interesting that the name of that particular oracle came to mean diviners in general who may have been inspired by Apollo, and that we have at least one sober historical account of that oracle being accurate.

There was obviously no trickery involved in this situation. The girl was clearly possessed by a spirit, which was recognized by the apostle Paul and the historian Luke. The spirit was clearly divining. We know, then, that divination was a real practice with real power.

Explanations

Now that we've seen some of the forms of divination mentioned in the Bible, and the widespread use of them and belief in them, the question arises: what is going on here? There are two possibilities. The first is that nothing more was going on than elaborate fraud.

The fraud theory says that the priests of the various pagan religions orchestrated the entire thing in order to gain political power. The people need to be convinced of the reality of the particular god or goddess in order to keep the tribute flowing. At least one historian finds it hard to believe, however, that deceit could operate so forcefully over a long period of time. "Imposture betrays itself, Falsehood never holds out. Besides, there were too many Witnesses, too many curious Spies, too many People whose Interest it was, not to suffer themselves to be deluded."[50] We also

50. Banier, *Mythology,* Vol. 1, 328.

have the account of the Pythoness in Acts, which was definitely not a work of fraud.

The second theory, that the oracles were accomplished by real spirits, is well set out by George Stanley Faber in his *Origin of Pagan Idolatry*. The objects of pagan worship, says Faber, were partly of the class of what the New Testament calls *demonia*. These *demonia* were not necessarily what we think of as devils, or evil spirits. "In the religious system of the old mythologists, Demons were the same as Hero-gods: and these Hero-gods were acknowledged to be the souls of eminent benefactors to mankind; who, after they had quitted this mortal sphere of existence, were worshipped as deities by a too grateful posterity."[51]

This idea of demons is also seen in Scripture. The words which are translated as "devils" or "demons" are *diamon* and *diamonion*. A *diamon* "signified, among pagan Greeks, an inferior deity, whether good or bad."[52] A likely derivation is from the root *da-*, "meaning to know, and hence means a knowing one."[53]

The idea of men being deified after death is also found in the writings of St. Augustine. When the Argive king Phoroneus died,

> his younger brother Phegous built a temple at his tomb, in which he was worshipped as God . . . because in his part of the kingdom . . . he had founded chapels for the worship of the gods, and had taught them to measure time by months and years and to that extent to keep count and reckoning of events."[54]

Augustine tells of similar origins of the Egyptian goddess Isis and god Serapis.

51. George Stanley Faber, *The Origin of Pagan Idolatry*, Vol. 1 (New York: Garland Publishing, 1984), 4.

52. Kohlenberger, *Vine's*, 283.

53. Ibid., 283.

54. Augustine, *City*, Book 18, Ch. 3.

Hesiod also makes this assertion:

> Now that the earth has gathered over this generation, these
> are called pure and blessed spirits; they live upon earth, and are
> good, they watch over mortal men and defend them from evil;
> they keep watch over lawsuits and hard dealings; they mantle
> themselves in dark mist and wander all over the country; they
> bestow wealth; for this right as of kings was given them.[55]

As to how these *demonia* could act as oracles, Faber says this:

> Since the devil is termed in Scripture the prince of the power
> of the air, and since the rapidity of a spirit's action must far
> exceed that which marks the action of a corporeal being; we
> may infer that Satan is able to convey intelligence respecting
> things present with inconceivable rapidity from one quarter of
> the world to another."[56]

His application is to the devil, but the principle is not limited
to him.

This ability to move rapidly from place to place would also
provide the ability to gather massive amounts of intelligence. Thus,
when the Delphic oracle was asked what Croesus was doing at that
moment, finding out was a simple task.

This intelligence gathering capability would also enable spirits
to make a pretense of prophecy. A spirit "who by the subtlety of his
nature possesses opportunities of knowing and combining things
present which never could be known and combined even by the
most consummate statesman, may draw more probable inferences
and guesses relative to futurity than a statesman could do."[57]

But even though the guesses were very informed, they were
still only guesses. That is why the prophecies of the oracles tended

---

55. Hesiod, *Works and Days*, lines 121–124.
56. Faber, *Origin*, Vol. 1, 7.
57. Ibid., 7–8.

to be vague, and capable of two quite different fulfillments. No matter what happened, the oracle would be right. Herodotus illustrates this in Croesus' dealings with the oracle at Delphi.

It is not necessary to believe that the souls of the dead actually became gods after death. It is possible that *demonia* encouraged this belief among people by deception.

We don't know how much freedom, if any, God gave to the dead once they were in Sheol, or Hades. The only biblical account we have is in 1 Samuel 28, and certain enchantments were necessary to bring up the prophet. Mythological accounts of Hades suggest that the dead were pretty well confined to the area.

But we can see that spirits, whoever they may be, could manipulate instruments of divination to tell an inquirer the current state of events, or how events might play themselves out.

In Augustine's testimony to the use of hydromancy by Numa, cited above, he says that what Numa saw in the water were "appearances whereby the demons made sport of him."[58]

Urim and Thummim/Lots

Two more biblical methods of divination need to be mentioned, but these are more by way of contrast, as they were approved by God and used righteously.

One such method was the Urim and Thummim. We have very little idea of what they were. The words themselves mean "light" (*urim*) and "perfection" (*thummim*).[59] They are first mentioned in Exodus 28:30, and they are connected with judgment: "And thou shalt put in the breastplate of judgment the Urim and the Thummim; and they shall be upon Aaron's heart, when he goeth in before the Lord: and Aaron shall bear the judgment of the children of Israel upon his heart before the Lord continually."

58. Augustine, *City*, Book 7, Ch. 35.
59. Smith, *Dictionary*, 719.

Their importance in judgment is made more clear in Numbers 27:21: "And he shall stand before Eleazar the priest, who shall ask counsel for him after the judgment of Urim before the Lord" (cf. 1 Sam. 28:6).

Although the Urim and Thummim are not mentioned expressly in 1 Samuel 23, they seem to be the focus of David's inquiry. Abiathar the priest was with David, and he had an ephod. David's questions are direct, and God's answers specific. Whether the answers came through the priest, or whether they came directly from the Urim and Thummim, is not clear.

One historian says the stones "gave out the oracular answer by preternatural illumination," which is possibly where the producers of the movie *King David* got the inspiration for Samuel's glowing stones.

However they worked, they were central to the deciding of important matters. After the return from Babylonian exile, chronicled in Ezra 2:63 and Nehemiah 7:65, several of the priestly families could not prove their heritage due to the loss of some of the records. They were excluded from partaking of the holy food "until a priest with Urim and Thummim should arise."

The other approved method was by the casting of lots. Exactly what procedure was followed and how the result was determined is unknown, but several cultures use lots.

It should be noted that the Israelites did not think of lots as random or chance decisions as we do. The way the lots came out was wholly determined by God. "The lot is cast into the lap; but the whole disposing thereof is of the Lord" (Prov. 16.33).

While the process is never explained, several examples are given. Lots determined the inheritance of the tribes of Israel (Num. 26:55–56); chose people out for judgement (1 Sam. 14:41–42); and chose church officers (Acts 1:26). There is no explanation as to when the lots were used, and when Urim and Thummim were to be consulted, but apparently they were equally valid and the ends were the same.

Conclusion

We can see, then, that an understanding of the creation existed at the time the Bible was written that is completely foreign to our way of thinking. The ancients understood that there was a whole realm of existence which could interact with man. When we begin to grasp how they saw the world, much biblical history is opened up to us.

The conclusion drawn from all of this is that the prohibitions in Deuteronomy against divination held a real threat to God's people. Not only a threat that they would fall away from Him, but that they would follow the other gods of the pagan nations. Whether, after the advent of Christ, we still need to be wary of an antagonistic spiritual realm is a matter of debate. But the test of true divination, whether from god or man, should always be that set forth by God in Deuteronomy 18:22: "When a prophet speaketh in the name of the Lord, if the thing follow not, nor come to pass, that is the thing which the Lord hath not spoken, but the prophet hath spoken it presumptuously: thou shalt not be afraid of him."

Bibliography

Banier, Abbè Antoine. *The Mythology and Fables of the Ancients Explained from History.* New York: Garland Publishing, Inc., 1976.

Faber, George Stanley, B.D. *The Origin of Pagan Idolatry.* New York: Garland Publishing, Inc., 1984.

Hesiod. *The Works and Days,* trans. R. Lattimore. Ann Arbor: University of Michigan Press, 1959.

Jamieson, Robert, A.R. Fausset, and David Brown. *A Commentary Critical, Experimental, and Practical on the Old and New Testaments.* Grand Rapids: William B. Eerdmans Publishing Company, 1976.

Josephus, Flavius. *The Works of Josephus,* ed. William Whiston. Lynn: Hendrickson Publishers, 1980.

Kohlenberger, John R., III, ed. *The Expanded Vine's Expository Dictionary of New Testament Words.* Minneapolis: Bethany House Publishers, 1984.

Loewe, Michael, and Carmen Blacker, eds. *Oracles and Divination.* Boulder: Shambhala, 1981.

Mackenzie, Donald A. *Myths of Babylon and Assyria.* London: The Gresham Publishing Company, Ltd., n.d.

Pember, G.H. *Earth's Earliest Ages.* Grand Rapids: Kregel Publishing, 1942.

Smith, William. *Smith's Bible Dictionary.* Old Tappan: Fleming H. Revell Company, 1982.

Summers, Montague. *The History of Witchcraft and Demonology.* Seacaucus: University Books, 1956.

The Bethany Parallel Commentary of the Old Testament. Minneapolis: Bethany House Publishers, 1985.

5

A BIBLICAL LOOK AT ANGELS

Christopher Schlect

I clearly remember my first encounter with an "angel." I was in seventh grade, at church camp, when a bunkmate pulled a photograph out of his Bible. It had been taken from an airplane window, with the clouds looking like a sea of fluff below the wing. The photo portrayed a ghostly white image of a person with outstretched arms hovering over the clouds outside the window.

"It's an angel," my friend said, and went on to tell, me how he had often doubted the Christian faith until this photo was developed. The picture had puzzled me until about a year later when I learned that camera film could be exposed twice. The very thought of angels is quite enticing to the imagination, and consequently popular thought concerning them often goes beyond the information we know about them from the Scriptures.

I once thought that angels, if they existed, were saints who, upon death, had cashed in their physical bodies in exchange for a robe, wings and a harp. Back then I was biblically illiterate. The Bible fails to offer concrete answers to many questions concerning angels, and some impatient theologians have fallen to the temptation of making claims about them that the text doesn't support. My intent is to offer a fair analysis of the information about angels that has been revealed through the Scriptures. This study falls far short of exhausting the subject, but hopefully it will clear the confusion in certain aspects.

Angels or Man?

In the original biblical languages, the words for "angel" are occupational rather than ontological. By this I mean that the words refer to what angels do rather than what they are. Unfortunately, in English they are usually understood ontologically. To say that an angel must be a celestial being is to say that a swimmer must be a person who somehow paddles along in water. In fact, the word "swimmer" may refer to a fish, duck, insect, amoeba or anything else that swims. The word "swimmer" doesn't necessarily refer to a human. Likewise, the word "angel" doesn't necessarily refer to a celestial being. Angel in the original Hebrew is (*malak*), and in the Greek it is (*angelos*).

Both words mean "sent one," and are often translated as "messenger," referring to one who is dispatched with a purpose, as in Philippians 2:25: "But I think it is necessary to send back to you Epaphroditus . . . who is also your messenger, whom you sent to take care of my needs." The word in question could just could just as well have been translated to English as "angel" instead of "messenger."

The Hebrew is used twice in 2 Kings 1:3, which could correctly be read as, "But the angel of the Lord said to Elijah the Tishbite, 'Go up and meet the angels of the king of Samaria.'" Similarly, Luke 7:24 refers to John's angels, his disciples. Sometimes the context isn't clear whether the word describes a celestial being or a man, which can create problems in translation.

For example, Proverbs 17:11 (NIV) says, "An evil man is bent only on rebellion; a merciless official will be sent against him." Merciless official is rendered "cruel messenger" in the KJV and RSV, but the passage could possibly refer to an angel of wrath because of the word it uses. Such possibilities must be taken into consideration and treated delicately before making assertions about the nature of angels. If one uses Scripture to make a point about celestial beings, one must be sure that the passage used actually refers to celestial beings rather than men.

Angels or God?

There are several theophanies in the Old Testament, i.e., instances when God Himself takes on physical form and reveals Himself to His people.

In Genesis 32, for example, Jacob sees God "face to face" (v. 30), a clear example of a theophany. This must be an early appearance of Christ, as it certainly isn't a presentation of God in His full glory as in Exodus 33. Regarding Jacob, the prophet Hosea says, "As a man he struggled with God. He struggled with the angel and overcame him" (Hos. 12:3–4). Here we see an early appearance of Christ, who is described as an angel, which is not uncommon in the Old Testament. There are many other places in the Old Testament where an "angel of the LORD" is clearly a theophany.[1]

After Manoah's encounter with an "angel of the LORD" in Judges 13, he says to his wife, "We are doomed to die! We have seen God!" (v. 22.)[2] Another example appears in Judges 6:11–20, where "angel of the LORD" and "LORD" are used interchangeably. This also occurs in Genesis 16:13, where an angel of the LORD is called "LORD" (that is, Jehovah). The account of Moses and the burning bush in Exodus 3, which I will discuss in more detail later, also substitutes "angel of the LORD" with "LORD."

Because these titles are used interchangeably in some places, we know that Christ can be referred to as an angel, one who is sent from God. There are several instances where an angel speaks with authority that seems far too lofty for a mere celestial being. For example, the angel of the Lord who speaks to Moses from the burning bush uses pronouns like "I" and "my" instead of "the LORD"

---

1. Colossians 2:9 says, "For in Christ the fullness of the Deity lives in bodily form."

2. In vv. 17–18, Manoah asks for the angel's name. The angel responds, "Why do you ask my name? It is wonderful." "Wonderful" here is the same word that appears in Isaiah 9:6: "And he will be called Wonderful, Counselor, Mighty God, Everlasting Father, Prince of Peace." With the exception of 2 Samuel 1:26, every other usage of this word in Scripture describes an attribute of God.

and "the LORD'S": "I have indeed seen the misery of my people in Egypt. I have heard them crying out because of their slave drivers, and I am concerned about their suffering. So I have come down to rescue them" (Exod. 3:7–8). Contrast this authoritative tone of God in the burning bush with the angel discussed in Zechariah 1, who, by his humble speech, shows that he is not God but one of God's celestial creations:

> Then the angel of the LORD said, "LORD Almighty, how long will you withhold mercy from Jerusalem and the towns of Judah, which you have been angry with these seventy years?" So the LORD spoke kind and comforting words to the angel who talked with me. (vv. 12–13)

When an angel speaks as if he has God's authority, it is a good clue that it may actually be God incarnate, the Christ. Consider the authority with which Jesus taught: "You have heard that it was said . . . But I tell you . . ." (Mt. 5:21, 27, 31, 33, 38, 40.) These factors must be taken into honest consideration when studying angels. Again, in order for one to make an assertion about celestial angels, one must be sure that the referenced passage is talking about a created, celestial being rather than its Creator.

Angelic Hierarchy

A third-century work entitled *Concerning Celestial Hierarchy*[3] was very influential in shaping medieval thought concerning angels. The author grouped different ranks of angels into three triads, creating a succession of nine beings neatly tucked within an authority

---

3. This and a companion work entitled Concerning Ecclesiastical Hierarchy were attributed by early theologians to Dionysius Areopagiticus (the Areopagite). The true origins of both works is unknown. Dionysius is known to have lived in the first century, as he is mentioned in Acts 17:34. Both of these works had enormous influence on medieval thought.

structure: Seraphim, Cherubim, and Thrones; Dominations, Virtues and Powers; Principalities, Archangels, and Angels. While it is clear that there is an authority structure in the heavens, this ancient author went far beyond the text to arrive at his conclusions.

For example, the only reference to thrones that isn't obviously referring to a king's or judge's chair (or a symbol of authority) is Colossians 1:16. Taking this passage to mean that thrones are created beings is to deny the overwhelming evidence in other passages which suggest otherwise. The revelation in the area of angelic hierarchy is limited, thus it is tempting to conceive of a hierarchy that is much more systematic than what Scripture demands. This fourth-century author got a bit carried away, and many medieval theologians followed in his footsteps. When discussing the hierarchy in the heavens, honest students of the Bible are left with saying, "It could be this way," or, "This option cannot be ruled out." To be much more elaborate, they must go beyond the Scriptures to support their claims. At the time when Christ said, "Do you think I cannot call on my Father, and he will at once put at my disposal more than twelve legions of angels?" (Mt. 26:53, NIV) the term "legion" usually referred to a principal unit of the Roman army comprising 3,000 to 6,000 foot soldiers with cavalry. These Roman legions had strictly defined chains of command.[4] Christ's reference to the angelic ranks as "legions" is evidence that a celestial hierarchy exists.

Before Christ's death He refused to call on twelve legions of angels, but when He returns He will command heavenly armies, as described in Revelation: "The armies of heaven were following him [Christ], riding on white horses and dressed in fine linen, white and clean . . . Then I saw the beast and the kings of the earth and their armies gathered together to make war against the rider on the horse and his army" (Rev. 19:14–19). Here we see Christ

---

4. Mark 5:15 gives us a glimpse of the authority structure in Roman legions.

at the top of the chain of command, leading a cavalry of angels into battle. The archangel Michael clearly has great authority in heaven. In Daniel 10:13, he is described as "one of the chief princes," and had come to help overcome the "king of Persia." In Revelation 12:7, Michael commands his own army of angels.

Though he is the only specifically mentioned archangel in the Bible,[5] the comment about him in Daniel 10:13 suggests the existence of other angels besides Michael. Other than Michael, the only angel who is mentioned by name is Gabriel, who stands "in the presence of God" (Lk. 1:19). In Daniel 8:16, Gabriel receives a command directly from the Lord. This information shows that Gabriel probably holds a high position among angels; perhaps he is an archangel.

Other angels are given special attention in scripture, such as the six angels in Revelation 14:6–20, and the seven angels of wrath discussed in Revelation 15–17. These angels have very important roles, but there is no chain of command among them that is clear in these chapters. They have been given much authority over the earth, but we don't know for sure if they have authority over other angels. There is obviously some sort of hierarchy among the angels in heaven. The fact that there are legions and armies of angels imply that this hierarchy is well defined. Throughout the Bible, angels are commissioned by God, thus showing that God is the "commander in chief." Many early theologians (and some modern ones) have constructed well-structured and detailed hierarchies in the heavens. Keep in mind that it is theologians who construct them, having embellished upon scriptural data. While the angelic hierarchy may indeed be very detailed, only a few of its details are revealed in the Scriptures.

---

5. Jude 9 and 1 Thessalonians 4:16 are the only places in the Bible where the word archangel is used.

Celestial Jurisdiction

Angels intervene in earthly affairs in many ways. For instance, God uses angels to carry messages to people, such as the angelic proclamation of Christ's birth to the shepherds in Luke 2. Angels are also used as agents of wrath, as demonstrated in the destruction of Jerusalem in 2 Samuel 24 (and 2 Chr. 21:15). The broad purpose of angels is summarized in Hebrews 11:14: "Are not all angels ministering spirits sent to serve those who will inherit salvation?" Angels are portrayed in Scripture as being assigned to particular tasks and having jurisdiction over certain portions of creation. In Psalm 78:49, for example, God releases a band of "destroying angels." From this we see that there are certain angels whose purpose is to destroy. Of course, destroying is not the ministry of every angel. In the Bible we see examples of angels who are warriors, angels who are heralds, angels who protect people, angels who tend to people's needs, and angels who do other things.

Clearly, there is some sort of division of labor among celestial beings. A friend of mine was recently in an auto accident in which his truck rolled over several times. He walked away from the accident without any significant injuries, and attributed this to an angel who sat in his lap. Though it is appropriate to thank the Sovereign Lord for the outcome of this accident, one cannot say for sure that my friend had an angel in his lap (which, of course, would be much more effective than any seat belt). However, such a possibility cannot be ruled out.

The Bible teaches that angels do guard people, which is clear in Psalm 91:11: "For he will give his angels charge of you to guard you in all your ways" (RSV). We can also see from this verse that angels are put in charge of us in the sense of jurisdiction. This is again evident in Matthew 18:10 where Jesus, in speaking of little children, mentions "their angels in heaven." These verses could possibly be describing a particular corporate body of celestial beings assigned to a particular group of people. Angels do guard us, but it is not clear that a certain angel is assigned to watch over one person for the duration of that person's life. God may call upon different angels to minister to a person as different needs arise.

The account of Peter's escape from prison in Acts 12 has been used by many to show that guardian angels have been assigned to specific individuals. While that may be true, making such an assertion from this passage requires a mishandling of the text. When Peter knocked at the door of Mary's house, he was mistaken for "his angel" (v. 15). It is important to remember that the angel could be a human messenger. The context is not clear enough to determine whether the passage refers to a man or a celestial being. Though the Bible doesn't answer all our questions concerning guardian angels, we can be sure that we are well guarded and properly ministered to.

Similar problems arise where the Scriptures speak of angels as having jurisdiction over institutions. In Revelation 2–3, for example, seven letters are written, each to an angel of a church. These angels could be human or celestial messengers—the context is not quite clear in pointing us to one conclusion over another. Daniel 9–10 mentions "princes" of particular nations. Michael is described as a prince, thus opening the possibility that other princes may in fact be angels (or fallen angels) who have jurisdiction over nations or regions.

It is clear that angels have some sort of system of jurisdiction over people. The system could be arranged according to geography, institutions, races or groups of people, or any combination thereof.

Ontology of Angels

Most of us have seen old artist's portrayals of angels. They are shown to be humanlike creatures with wings. Some have robes, some bear weapons and armor, and many just float around in the air for no apparent reason.[6] Concerning wings, there is nothing in the Bible that clearly suggests that angels have wings. They have been known to fly, such as when the angel Gabriel comes to Daniel in "swift flight" (Dan. 9:21). The Seraphim in the throne room of God do have wings, but this is no reason to suppose that angels have wings too. Angels and Seraphim are completely different beings. Angels often take on the form of humans, and are in fact sometimes described as men or mistaken for men.

Hebrews 13:2 says, "Do not forget to entertain strangers, for by so doing some people have entertained angels without knowing it."

However, it is clear that angels are not bound to the same limitations that humans are.

We have seen that they are capable of flying, appearing and disappearing, going into battle against evil supernatural powers, and destroying to a degree that is far beyond the capacity of any man. Angels do not operate according to natural laws, thus they are not limited by time and space as we understand time and space. However, the materialist, who sets his eyes only on the part of God's creation over which he has been given dominion, can think of reality only in terms of matter operating according to "natural laws." His reasoning follows like this: All reality operates within the parameters of time and space; since angels are not limited by time and space, then they either have no limitations or (more consistently) they don't exist. The latter conclusion is biblically unacceptable, as the Scriptures are clear in showing that angels do exist. The idea that angels are limitless, on the other hand, has been held by some who have tried to reconcile materialism with the Bible. If angels are limitless, then angels would be God. There are natural limitations placed upon angels and other celestial beings that are not the same limitations we are bound to.

6. And it is amazing to realize how much of our cosmology has been adopted from cartoons!

Though celestial beings may know more than we do, they are not omniscient. For they did not know God's secret wisdom that is mentioned in 1 Corinthians 2 and in 1 Peter 1:12. Though angels are more powerful than we are, they are not omnipotent. If angels were omnipotent, then the angel in Daniel 10 would not have been detained for twenty one days. Though God's angels are good, they are not omnibenevolent, for some angels have fallen.

Hebrews 1:7 says, "He will make his angels winds, his servants flames of fire," referring to the unique ontology of God's celestial messengers. The passage goes on to say that, though angels transcend human limitations, they are not as great as Christ: "To which of the angels did God ever say, 'Sit at my right hand until I make your enemies a footstool for your feet?'" (v. 13).

It is tempting for humans to worship or pray to anyone or anything that is superhuman. We are awestruck by anything that is out of our dominion. We must remember that the awesome power and splendor of angels does not warrant praise and worship unto them, but rather unto the One who created them. Anything else is a form of idolatry.

Angels and Spiritual Warfare

Ephesians 6:12 says: "For our battle is not against flesh and blood, but against the rulers, against the authorities, against the powers of this dark world and against the spiritual forces of evil in the heavenly realms." Upon conversion, the sinner's carnal nature is put to death; he is given new life in the Holy Spirit. Consequently, there is nothing in the Christian's nature that draws him toward sin. On the contrary, obedience comes naturally (but not always easily) to those who have been crucified and raised to new life with Christ. This verse in Ephesians reminds us that a Christian's battle against sin is not waged against himself, but against the "powers of this dark world" and the "spiritual forces of evil in the heavenly realms." To be effective in this battle, Christians must "put on the full armor of God" and "pray in the Spirit on all occasions" (vv. 13–20). The importance of angels in this battle cannot be overemphasized. Our humanness makes us weaker than our spiritual enemies.

We simply were not created with the same power and abilities that heavenly beings have. If we go off into battle on our own, we will certainly suffer casualties. Instead we are to pray for Divine assistance, acknowledging that by ourselves we are in over our heads.

We are not to pray to the angels, for they answer only to God. We are to pray to the One who sends the angels. Daniel 9–10 contains an exciting account of spiritual warfare. The bulk of chapter 9 records Daniel praying as he acknowledges the sovereignty of God and confesses his own sin and the sin of his people. With this humble attitude he petitions God for the restoration of Jerusalem. The results are recorded in verses 20–23:

> While I was speaking and praying, confessing my sin and the sin of my people Israel and making my request to the Lord my God for his holy hill—while I was still in prayer, Gabriel, the man I had seen in the earlier vision, came to me in swift flight about the time of the evening sacrifice. He instructed me and said to me, "Daniel, I have now come to give you insight and understanding. As soon as you began to pray, an answer was given, which I have come to tell you."

As soon as Daniel prayed, an answer was given and the angel Gabriel was dispatched to carry out the answer. This shows that prayer yields results as God responds by sending an angel. This does not mean that God always responds to prayer by dispatching angels, but when it is appropriate, He will do so. When we pray, we must trust that the Lord will answer appropriately—He knows if, when, where, and how His angels ought to be sent out. God is the one who dictates the policy of heaven, and we have a responsibility to pray. Prayer is critical in spiritual warfare.

In chapter 10, we catch a glimpse of the spiritual battle from an angel's perspective. The angel that is sent to Daniel is detained by "the Price of the Persian kingdom" for twenty-one days until Michael comes to help him. After speaking with Daniel, he returns to fight against the prince of Persia, and warns about the coming of the prince of Greece. There is obviously significant tension between the forces of good and evil in the spiritual realm, and God's angels are involved.

Because these powers, both good and evil, have such great influence on earthly affairs, Paul tells us to "pray in the Spirit on all occasions with all kinds of prayers and requests . . . be alert and always keep on praying for all the saints." When we pray like this, God will dispatch all the forces necessary to help us carry out His will.

There is so much popular mythology surrounding aft that many people have grouped them with cyclopes and Caspar the friendly ghost. Many who understand that the Bible acknowledges the existence of angels feel compelled to accept along with them characteristics that are mythological and not biblical.

Those who hold the Scriptures in high esteem are concerned about knowing the truth and rejecting what is false, including the truth about celestial beings. Rather than apologizing for believing in something as "silly" as angels, we should rejoice in the truth, which we find through sober exegesis. To be correct in our understanding of angels, we must be willing to admit that there are many questions that have uncertain answers. This should not frustrate us. The Father has created glorious, powerful beings to minister to us, and He deserves our thanks and praise for what He has made.

6

SATYRS, LILITH, & LUNATICS

Wesley Callihan

Two major difficulties face the modern student of Scripture trying to understand a text produced in an ancient culture. One is that of grasping the historical, cultural, and geographical context of the Bible; the other is trying to shed the deadening materialistic baggage the modern Western world has lumbered him with. By materialism I mean the denial of that supernaturalism which is fundamental to a biblical worldview, and which was universal in the ancient world.

The first difficulty is not at all insurmountable; there are books. The second very nearly is, however, considering the interpretational contortions many biblical scholars practice when faced with anything in the Scriptures for which the modern world provides no adequate mental category. I say "adequate" because it does provide for those things—it calls them products of primitive superstition or mythology.

As a result, and because Christians make the mistake of wanting to be acceptable to the modern age, where such things occur in Scripture they are translated into something palatable to modern taste, if at all possible; where it is not possible the Bible helps talk about the "difficulties of interpretation," and anyway the vast majority of Bible readers pass over those places without noticing anything strange.

Satyrs

Two such instances occur in the same passage in a prophetic book of the eighth century B.C.: the satyrs and lilith of Isaiah 34. In his prophecy against Edom, Isaiah says,

> It shall be an habitation of dragons, and a court for owls. The wild beasts of the desert shall also meet with the wild beasts of the island, and the satyr shall cry to his fellow; the screech owl also shall rest there, and find for herself a place of rest. (vv. 13–14)

This passage from the Authorized Version presents an odd problem which is only partially solved in some newer translations. The odd part is that one's attention is attracted to the exotic word "dragon," which here most likely means simply "jackal" (although in other Old Testament passages something very like what we mean by "dragon" is intended), while we pass over the innocuous "screech owl" without a thought. The concept underlying the Hebrew word so poorly translated by "owl," however, is so exotic that for many scholars it "presents great difficulties of interpretation."[1] The intermediate word "satyr" is properly translated but most readers haven't a clue about the definition.

There are four other places in the Old Testament which refer to satyrs and will be helpful in understanding the concept. Isaiah says in an earlier prophecy about Babylon (13:21) that "satyrs shall dance there" (on its ruins). In Leviticus 17:7, (roughly 1200–1400 B.C.), the Lord tells the Israelites through Moses that they must "no more offer their sacrifices unto devils, after whom they have gone a whoring." The word translated as "devil" is "satyr." Second Chronicles 11:15 says that Rehoboam, Solomon's son, ruling in the tenth century B.C., set up "priests for the high places, and for the devils,

---

1. J. D. Douglas, ed., *New Bible Dictionary*, 2d ed. (Wheaton: Tyndale House, 1982), 701.

and for the calves which he had made." The word for "devils" again is "satyrs." In the seventh century B.C., Josiah "brake down the high places of the gates that were in the entering in of the gate of Joshua the governor of the city" (2 Kgs. 23:8). Now we know this means he was demolishing idols but, although most translations of the Old Testament use it, this phrasing doesn't make sense. However, the New English Bible says he "dismantled the hill-shrines of the demons in front of the gate of Joshua." The Masoretic Text of the Old Testament uses the word "satyr" and that is what the NEB translates as "demons," but some manuscripts contain a scribal error in which a minor slip has resulted in the reading "gate," the two Hebrew words being similar orthographically.[2]

Satyrs are understood by every culture that knew of them to be creatures with goat-like characteristics; usually they have the body of a man (although there are females, called "satyra") and the legs of a goat (or occasionally another animal). The Hebrew word which is transliterated as "satyr" is related to the word "hairy," and is closely related to the word for "he-goat"; however, in the five passages identified above, the usage of the word is distinctly to be interpreted as a satyr as classically understood, or a demon with goat-like characteristics.[3]

In the Leviticus, Chronicles, and Kings references, the context indicates clearly that the satyrs were objects of idolatry. Therefore, satyrs were believed not only to exist, but to be minor gods, or "demons" in the classical sense; that is, they were malevolent beings with some specially supernatural quality. All standard translations recognize this by using words such as devil, demon, or idol to translate the word "satyr." Furthermore, the passages span at least six hundred years, so that belief in (and worship of) satyrs was not a short-lived aberration; neither was it isolated geographically,

2. Ibid., 1075.

3. Francis Brown, S. R. Driver, and Charles A. Briggs, *A Hebrew and English Lexicon of the Old Testament* (Oxford: Clarendon Press, 1907), 972.

for the ancient Greeks and Romans included them in their stock of "mythological" creatures for a thousand years. It is possible that goats simply became the object of superstition due to the scapegoat law,[4] but not likely because so many other cultures believed in satyrs as well.

The Isaiah passages do not refer to idolatry, however; they simply affirm by their reference the truth of the existence of such creatures. Most, but not all, common translations read "goat" here, where the KJV says "satyr," but this is because there is not the contextual pressure that the passages on idolatry apply; however, even in the ones that use "goats" a footnote is often supplied pointing out that "satyr" is the word they are translating, and that the "demon" meaning cannot be ignored. We can hardly use as an objection here the possibility of superstitious development of the scapegoat into a demonic being; Isaiah would have been the first man to condemn such a falsehood, especially if it tended toward idolatry. One might object that this is poetry and so we needn't take literally a reference to a mythological creature. But to call it a mythological creature is begging the question, and the poetry issue is beside the point; even in poetry, there are indications about whether we ought to understand what is being said as literal or symbolic. Here a natural reading doesn't seem to call for a symbolic interpretation; the only pressure for a symbolic interpretation comes from a prior disbelief in supernatural creatures.

Lilith

The materialist viewpoint causes even more trouble when we discover what the word in Isaiah 34:14 translated "screech owl" really is. "Lilith" is the transliterated Hebrew word, and there is only one possible meaning for it. It is the name of a female night-demon

4. Douglas, *Dictionary*, 1075, 1077. See also Leviticus 16.
5. Brown, *Lexicon*, 539.

referred to in ancient Babylonian records; the word (and so, presumably, the concept) came probably from the Assyrian *lilitu*[5] when the Jews were under the influence of that language in their captivity. The *New Bible Dictionary* says, "some scholars regard [lilith] as the equivalent of the English vampire."[6] Although there may be a touch of sarcasm in the phrase, the analogy may be very accurate.

On a limestone amulet discovered in the Near East, and dating from approximately one hundred years after Isaiah (seventh century B.C.), is inscribed an incantation for the purpose of repelling female flying demons from dwellings. These creatures are called the "stranglers" because they were believed to cause the death of infants and small children.[7] The word used in the original language is the same as that which Isaiah uses, and the additional descriptions ("strangler," "female demon," "female flying demon") aid in identifying the nature of the creatures which frightened the Babylonians enough to obtain these amulets.

There can be no objection to the assertion that knowledge of the lilith was picked up from the Babylonians, along with the word for it, but this doesn't speak to the issue of the truth or falsehood of the belief. For Isaiah to use this word without redefinition was to validate the meaning which he certainly knew his hearers or readers would apply to it.

As late as the Christian era, the belief in lilith remained popular. Aramaic Incantation Bowls found in Babylon, and dating from the third to the sixth century A.D., have images and descriptions of demons inscribed on them, along with incantations about their binding; they commonly refer to "King Solomon, Son of David" and his seal ring, and show a bound demon surrounded by the incantation which binds it. One says, "bound is the bewitching

6. Douglas, *Dictionary*, 701.

7. James B. Pritchard, ed., *Ancient Near Eastern Texts Relating to the Old Testament* (Princeton: Princeton University Press, 1969), 658.

Lilith who haunts the house of Zakoy," then repeats the phrase five times with descriptions of the bonds on her head, nose, mouth, neck, hands, and feet.[8] The incantation and accompanying image indicate the nature of the creature referred to: it is female, it has shape roughly reminiscent of a human form, and it is malevolent, haunting demon. The word used in the incantation is the same as that used in the Isaiah passage.

In the Testament of Solomon (written probably in the third century A.D.) in the Pseudepigrapha, there is a description of a female demon named Obyzouth who is interrogated by Solomon; she is described as having "disheveled" and "savage" hair, and "her body was darkness." She explains that she spends every night seeking women about to give birth so that she might strangle the newborn infants. The disheveled hair is reminiscent of the Greek Medusa, the sight of whom was deadly, and the connection is more than coincidental, for the Jews knew of this character and a burial amulet with a Medusa on it has been found on a Jewish corpse.[9] Solomon inquires of another female demon, named Onoskelis, who lives in cliffs, caves, and ravines, travels by night (literally, by means of the moon), and perverts or strangles men. She is a female satyr, because although she has the body of a beautiful woman she has mule's legs; nevertheless, she is identical in behavior to the liliths.[10] In the Jewish Targum that interprets 1 Kings 4:33, Solomon is described as having mastery over the demons, and liliths are named specifically.[11] The significance of these late Jewish magical traditions is that it corroborates the definition of lilith obtained from the ancient Babylonians and used *in situ* by Isaiah. And the obvious implication is that if Isaiah's use of the concept lends it

8. James H. Charlesworth, ed., *The Old Testament Pseudepigrapha*, Vol. 1 (Garden City: Doubleday, 1983), 1.967, note 5p.

9. Ibid., 1.973–74.

10. Ibid., 1.964–5.

11. Ibid., 1.947–8.

credence, then the later Jewish magical traditions may have been more than mere "cabalistic" superstition.

Many modern translations translate the word "owl"; some commentators object to such translations on the grounds that the owl names used are not those of inhabitants of those desert regions; however, though this may be true, it entirely misses the point. There is absolutely no evidence linguistically for such a translation. It is very clear that the creature referred to is best understood as the female night demon the Babylonians knew as lilith. Again, the only possible objection to a literal understanding would be the poetic character of the prophecies, but this isn't a strong argument for the reason stated earlier; we should also consider that since one of Isaiah's purposes in prophesying was to condemn the massive adoption of pagan ways from the surrounding nations, it would be very much out of character for him to accommodate himself to this belief if it were a false one.

Lunacy, Possession, and Epilepsy

> They brought unto him . . . those which were possessed with devils, and those which were lunatick. (Mt. 4:24)

The English word "lunatic," based on the Latin *luna* ("moon") literally means someone who is periodically insane, or otherwise mentally affected, in relation to changes of the moon; that is, someone who is "moonstruck." It is used hereafter in this strict sense, not in the modern loose sense (that is, "crazy"). The word is singularly appropriate in the above text, for the Greek word it translates means precisely the same thing. This Greek word is used only one other time in the New Testament, in Matthew 17:14–21, where we are told of a man who brings his son to Jesus to be healed, "for he is *lunatick* and sore vexed: for ofttimes he falleth into the fire, and oft into the water."

In this passage, the child is cured when Jesus casts out a demon, so that although we are not told that demon possession is related to the boy's fits, it seems clear enough after the exorcism. Furthermore, what appears to be the same story is told also in Mark 9:14–29 and Luke 9:37–42, and there it explicitly says that the spirit (demon) causes the fits: it "taketh him . . . and teareth him"—lunacy is not mentioned at all. The strength of the connection between lunacy and demon possession in the Matthew 17 account is difficult to assess, because although if the stories in the three synoptic gospels tell of the same event then the boy in Matthew 17 was "moonstruck" *and* demon possessed, still we cannot tell whether this implies that lunacy and demon possession are causally or merely coincidentally related in the boy. In other words, is he "lunatick and sore vexed (by that lunacy)" or is he "lunatick and (also) sore vexed (by a demon)"? We can certainly say that lunacy and demon possession are not necessarily the same thing, for in the first passage quoted (Mt. 4:24) the two are mentioned separately: "those which were possessed with devils, and those which were lunatick."

Most modern translations use the word "epileptic" in place of "lunacy" in the two Matthew passages. There are two points to be made about the use of this term in connection with these accounts. First, we may not *substitute* it for the *demon possession* in Matthew 17, Mark 9, and Luke 9. It is a modern replacement for the term "lunacy." Epilepsy can only be substituted for demon possession if lunacy and demon possession are the same thing. If they are, then we find ourselves asserting that epilepsy and spirit possession are the same thing. We are not allowed to say demon possession was "really" epilepsy, for the wording is clear—Jesus cast out a demon. But if we keep the concept of possession and say it is epilepsy, then epilepsy is "really" possession—there is no middle road—and modern treatment of epileptics had better take a look at the old business of exorcism.

Second, if we accept that possession and lunacy are different things (even if related), and that lunacy (not demon possession) is epilepsy, it doesn't remove the necessity of dealing with the fact that the malady was seen as somehow related to a celestial body. To call it epilepsy is only to further describe, not to explain it. There clearly was a view in the ancient world that some kinds of mental instability were related to the influence of the moon. Psalm 121:6 says, in reference to the Lord's help, "The sun shall not smite thee by day, nor the moon by night." This "suggests that [the moon] was recognized as capable of affecting the mind."[12] It would be difficult to assert, as one can about the sun, that it implies a physical problem with the light rays; who ever complained about the heat of the moon?

Nevertheless, the strongest argument for the assertion that the moon exerts an influence which produces in some people temporary mental unsoundness, of varying degrees and with varying physical manifestations, is that the Bible assumes the truth of that assertion by using, without redefinition, the word which encapsulates it.

We cannot assert that epilepsy is lunacy—that is, a mental disturbance produced by the moon and its changes. We can assert, however, that there really is epilepsy and there really is lunacy. The moon's influence may be a factor in epilepsy; on the other hand, it may be a factor in other mental problems (such as manic-depression, or schizophrenia) as well, or perhaps instead. Some mental problems can be adequately explained by physiological problems (such as an infant with brain damage that causes almost constant minor seizures), while others cannot.

The connection between moon madness and spirit possession is strengthened by two facts: one, that Jesus's exorcism of the

12. Douglas, *Dictionary*, 793, and cf. *Oxford English Dictionary*, "moonstruck" (John Simpson and Edmund Weiner, eds. [Oxford: Clarendon Press, 1989]).

devils cured, apparently completely, the lunatic; and second, that celestial bodies can be said biblically to be associated with intelligence, with spiritual beings (argument to be found elsewhere). In the Testament of Solomon in the Pseudepigrapha (c. A.D. 300), a female night demon (a lilith) who seduces and strangles is said to travel in the moon; although this is certainly not an authoritative text, it indicates the prevalence of the belief not only that spirits were associated with celestial bodies, but that they were sometimes malevolent. We must acknowledge that at least part of that belief is corroborated scripturally, and the Bibles silence on the remainder leaves no authoritative grounds for assertions of truth or falsehood.

www.ingramcontent.com/pod-product-compliance
Lightning Source LLC
Chambersburg PA
CBHW060329050426
42449CB00011B/2708